LangChain
Crash Course

Greg Lim

Copyright © 2024 Greg Lim
All rights reserved.

LangChain Crash Course: Build OpenAI LLM Powered Apps

Copyright © 2023 by Greg Lim

All rights reserved.
No part of this book may be reproduced in any form or by any electronic or mechanical means including information storage and retrieval systems, without permission in writing from the author. The only exception is by a reviewer, who may quote short excerpts in a review.

Second Edition: April 2024

Table of Contents

PREFACE 5

CHAPTER 1: INTRODUCTION 7

CHAPTER 2: WHAT IS LANGCHAIN 9

CHAPTER 3: HOW DOES LANGCHAIN WORK 13

Chapter 4: Installation, Setup and our First LangChain App 19

CHAPTER 5: CONNECTING TO OPENAI LLM 25

CHAPTER 6: PROMPT TEMPLATES 29

CHAPTER 7: SIMPLE CHAINS 33

CHAPTER 8: SEQUENTIAL CHAINS 37

CHAPTER 9: AGENTS 43

CHAPTER 10: CHAT WITH A DOCUMENT 49

CHAPTER 11: ADDING MEMORY (CHAT HISTORY) 57

CHAPTER 12: OUTPUTTING THE CHAT HISTORY 61

CHAPTER 13: UPLOADING CUSTOM DOCUMENTS 65

CHAPTER 14: LOADING DIFFERENT FILE TYPES 73

CHAPTER 15: CHAT WITH YOUTUBE 79

ABOUT THE AUTHOR 86

Preface

About this book

In this book, we take you on a fun, hands-on and pragmatic journey to learning LangChain. You'll start building your first LangChain app within minutes. Every chapter is written in a bite-sized manner and straight to the point as I don't want to waste your time (and most certainly mine) on the content you don't need.

In the course of this book, we will cover:
- Chapter 1: Introduction
- Chapter 2: What is LangChain
- Chapter 3: How Does LangChain Work
- Chapter 4: Installation, Setup and Our First LangChain App
- Chapter 5: Connecting to OpenAI LLM
- Chapter 6: Prompt Templates
- Chapter 7: Simple Chains
- Chapter 8: Sequential Chains
- Chapter 9: Agents
- Chapter 10: Chat with a Document
- Chapter 11: Adding Memory (Chat History)
- Chapter 12: Outputting the Chat History
- Chapter 13: Uploading Custom Documents
- Chapter 14: Loading Different File Types
- Chapter 15: Chat with YouTube

The goal of this book is to teach you LangChain in a manageable way without overwhelming you. We focus only on the essentials and cover the material in a hands-on practice manner for you to code along.

Working Through This Book

This book is purposely broken down into short chapters where the development process of each chapter will center on different essential topics. The book takes a practical hands on approach to learning through practice. You learn best when you code along with the examples in the book.

Requirements

You should have basic programming knowledge.

Getting Book Updates

To receive updated versions of the book, subscribe to our mailing list by sending a mail to support@i-ducate.com. I try to update my books to use the latest version of software, libraries and will update the codes/content in this book. So, do subscribe to my list to receive updated copies!

Code Examples

You can obtain the source code of the completed project by contacting support@i-ducate.com

Online Course

If you are a more visual learner & learn better from absorbing this book's content through an online course, you can access the book's online course by contacting support@i-ducate.com and providing a proof of purchase.

The course content is the same as this book. So, if learning through books is your preferred way of learning, skip this. But if you prefer to learn from videos (and you want to hear my voice), contact me.

CHAPTER 1: INTRODUCTION

In recent times, you would probably have heard of many AI applications, one of them being chatpdf.com.

On this website, you can upload your own PDF. After uploading, you can have a conversation by asking questions about your PDF, and the site will provide you with the answers.

So, for example, if I upload the US Constitution to this website and it processes it, I can ask questions like, "What is the purpose of the Constitution of the United States?" or "How is the House of Representatives composed and elected?"

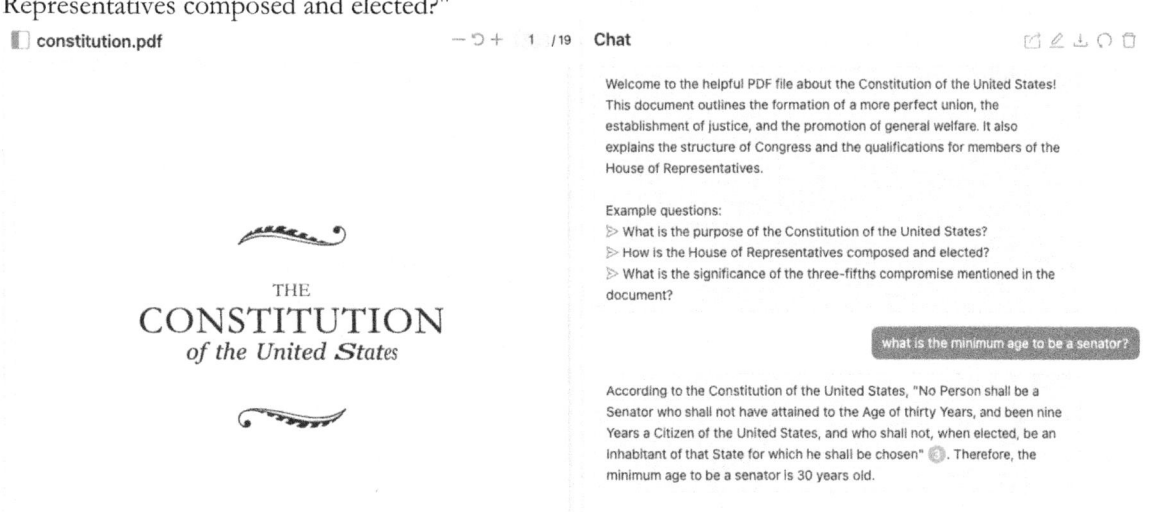

I might also pose my own questions, such as, "What is the minimum age to be a senator?"

The website responds that the minimum age to be a senator is 30 years old:

> what is the minimum age to be a senator?

According to the Constitution of the United States, "No Person shall be a Senator who shall not have attained to the Age of thirty Years, and been nine Years a Citizen of the United States, and who shall not, when elected, be an Inhabitant of that State for which he shall be chosen" [3]. Therefore, the minimum age to be a senator is 30 years old.

If I click a feature to "scroll to page three", it will show the part of the text from which the answer was derived.

No Person shall be a Senator who shall not have attained to the Age of thirty Years, and been nine Years a Citizen of the United States, and who shall not, when elected, be an Inhabitant of that State for which he shall be chosen.

The Vice President of the United States shall be President of the Senate, but shall have no Vote, unless they be equally divided.

The Senate shall chuse their other Officers, and also a President pro tempore, in the Absence of the Vice President, or when he shall exercise the Office of President of the United States

Now, if you want to develop an application like this, how should you go about it? Many developers choose to use a technology called "LangChain". In this course, we will introduce LangChain and demonstrate how to integrate it with large language models, like OpenAI GPT, to develop these amazing apps.

CHAPTER 2: WHAT IS LANGCHAIN

What is LangChain?

If you refer to the LangChain documentation (https://python.langchain.com/), it states that LangChain is a framework for developing applications powered by language models.

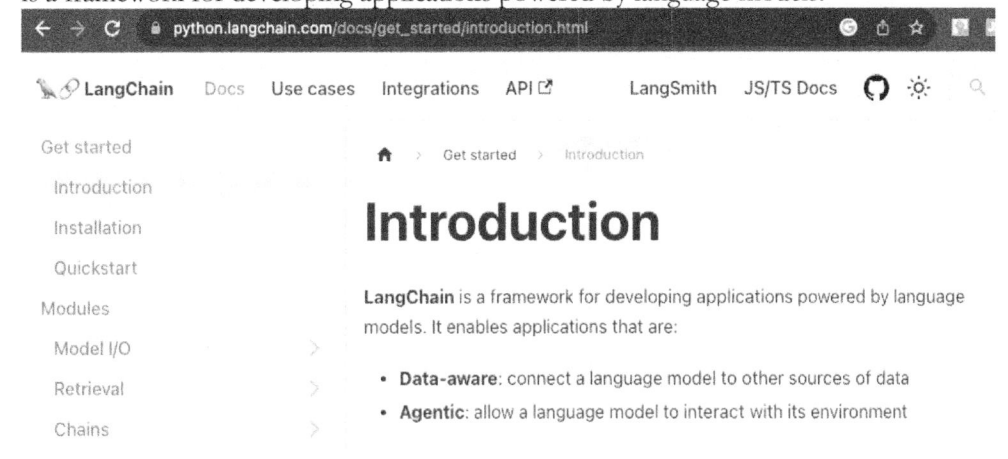

This means we can utilize language models like OpenAI's GPT-4 in conjunction with external data to develop AI applications.

The LangChain framework is available both as a Python and a JavaScript package. In this course, we'll be focusing on Python.

Now, if we inquire about the limitations of ChatGPT, what do we find?

> what limitations do you have

As of my last training data in September 2021, there are several limitations to keep in mind when interacting with me:

Content Limitations

1. **Outdated Information**: My training only includes data up to September 2021, so any events or developments that have occurred after that date won't be part of my knowledge base.
2. **Generalized Knowledge**: While I strive for accuracy, I can't guarantee that my responses are entirely accurate or up-to-date. Always consult multiple sources when making important decisions based on information I provide.
3. **Medical, Legal, Financial Advice**: I'm not a licensed professional in medical, legal, or financial fields. Any information I provide in these areas should not be considered professional advice.
4. **Specific Personal Advice**: I can't offer personalized advice or opinions as I don't have access to personal data (and don't have the capability to understand or analyze it in the same way a human would).

Firstly, we know that its training data only extends up to September 2021. As a result, it might not be cognizant of events or information post that date. Additionally, it cannot access real-time information or updates from the Internet.

Privacy is another concern. ChatGPT does not have access to personal data concerning individuals, companies, or even your own business documents.

This is where LangChain comes into play. It enables linking of the language models to various external data sources, whether it's personal documents, real-time updates from the Internet, or other pertinent data. For instance, it can integrate information from sources like Wikipedia and Google.

This attribute is referred to as being "data aware":

Introduction

LangChain is a framework for developing applications powered by language models. It enables applications that are:

- **Data-aware**: connect a language model to other sources of data
- **Agentic**: allow a language model to interact with its environment

With LangChain, we can seamlessly connect a robust language model, such as GPT-4, to our preferred data sources.

But LangChain's prowess isn't confined to just being data aware.

It is also "agent aware" or as mentioned here, "Agentic". LangChain can allow a language model to interact with its environment by executing actions, like web search, sending an email, performing mathematical operations, or even executing Python code, LangChain's agents can determine the appropriate action to execute. We will look at these in the course of this book.

CHAPTER 3: HOW DOES LANGCHAIN WORK

How does LangChain work?

Let's consider our initial example where we upload the US Constitution PDF and pose questions to it. In this scenario, LangChain compiles the data from the PDF and organizes it.

Although we've mentioned a PDF, the data source could be diverse: a text file, a Microsoft Word document, a YouTube transcript, a website, and more. LangChain collates this data, subsequently dividing it into manageable chunks. Once segmented, these chunks are saved in a vector store:

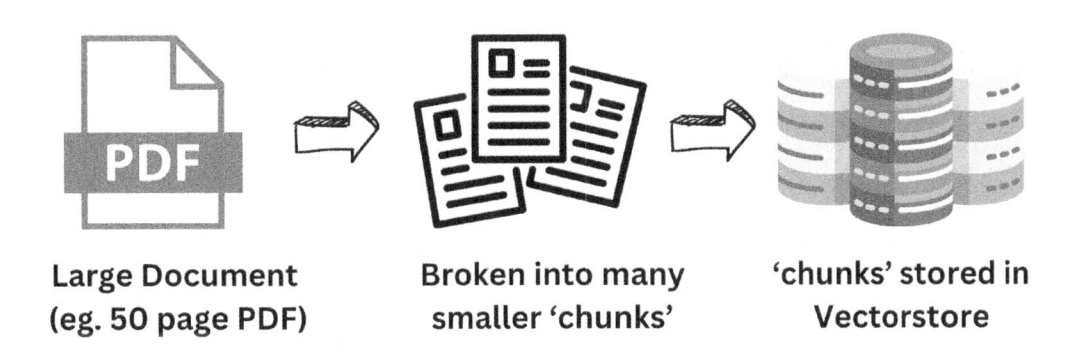

Large Document (eg. 50 page PDF) → **Broken into many smaller 'chunks'** → **'chunks' stored in Vectorstore**

For illustration, let's say our PDF contains the text displayed on the left, termed the text corpus. LangChain will segment this text into smaller chunks.

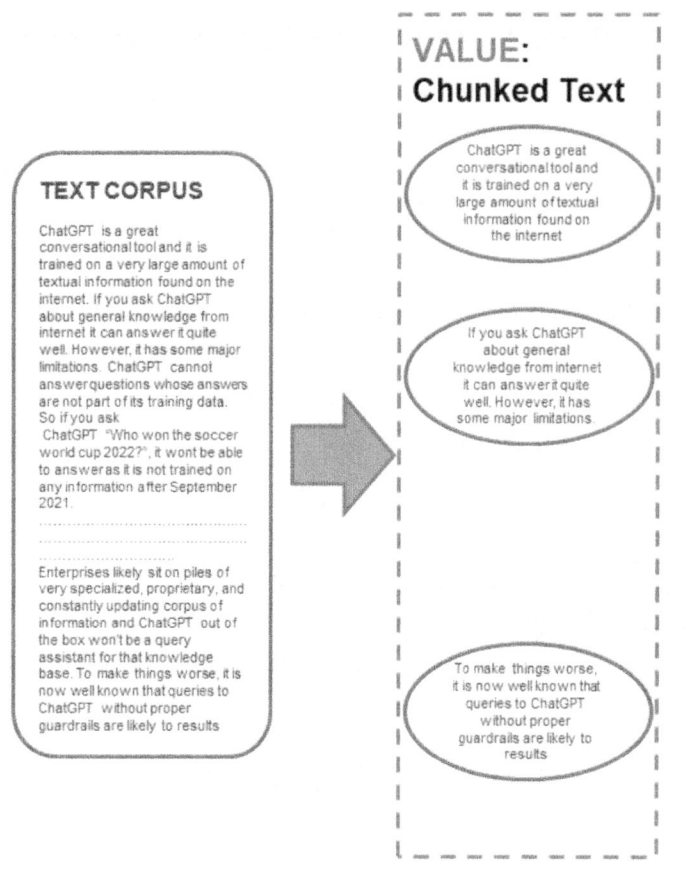

(source: medium.com/thirdai-blog/understanding-the-fundamental-limitations-of-vector-based-retrieval-for-building-llm-powered-48bb7b5a57b3)

For instance, one chunk might read "GPT is a great conversational tool...", followed by "if you ask ChatGPT about general knowledge...". These are distinct sections of the chunked text.

Our large language model (LLM) will then transform this chunked text into embeddings.

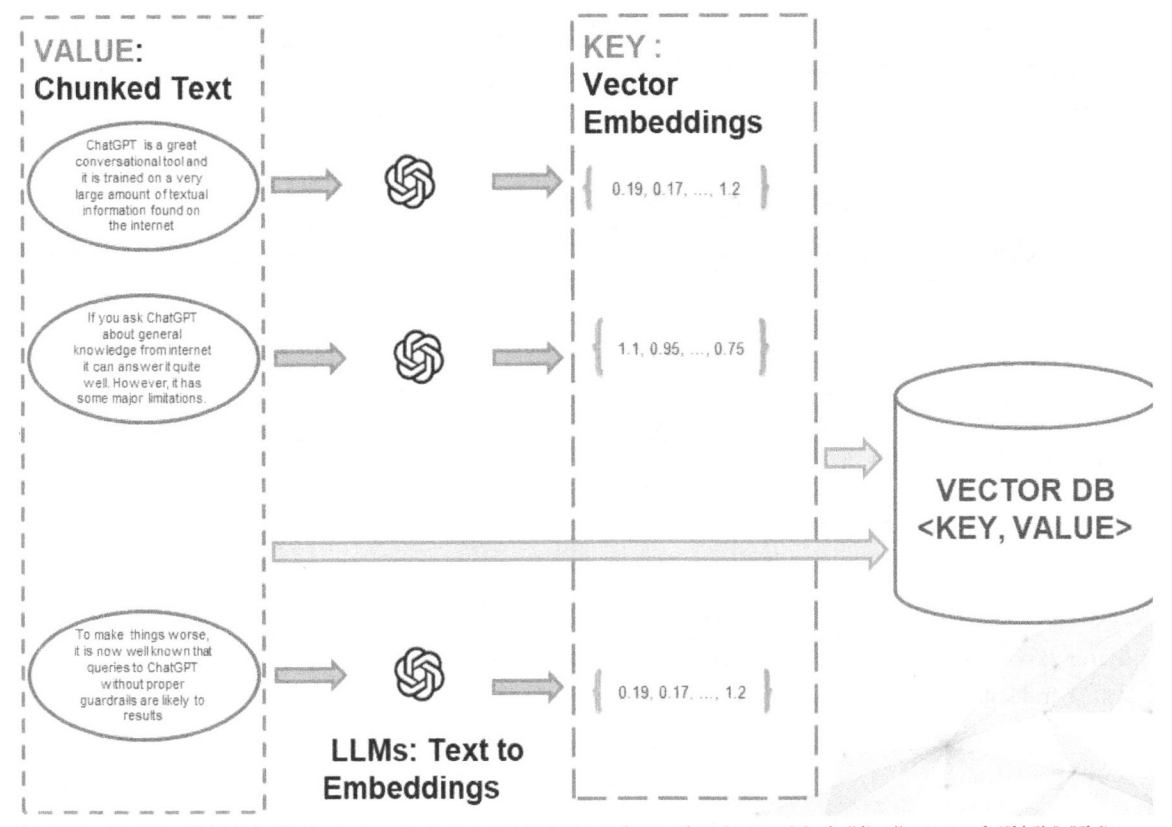

(source: medium.com/thirdai-blog/understanding-the-fundamental-limitations-of-vector-based-retrieval-for-building-llm-powered-48bb7b5a57b3)

Embeddings are simply numerical representations of the data. The text chunk is rendered into a numerical vector, which is then stored in a vector store/database.

You might question the necessity of this conversion. Data is multifaceted, encompassing text, images, audio, and video. To assign meaningful interpretations to such diverse content forms, they must be translated into numerical vectors.

This translation from chunks to embeddings employs various machine learning algorithms. These algorithms categorize the data, and the resultant classifications are saved in the vector database.

Querying the Vector Store and Generating a Completion with a LLM

When a user poses a question, this inquiry is also converted into an embedding, a numerical vector representation. This vector is juxtaposed with existing vectors in the database to perform a similarity search. The database identifies vectors most akin to the query and retrieves the chunks from which these vectors originated.

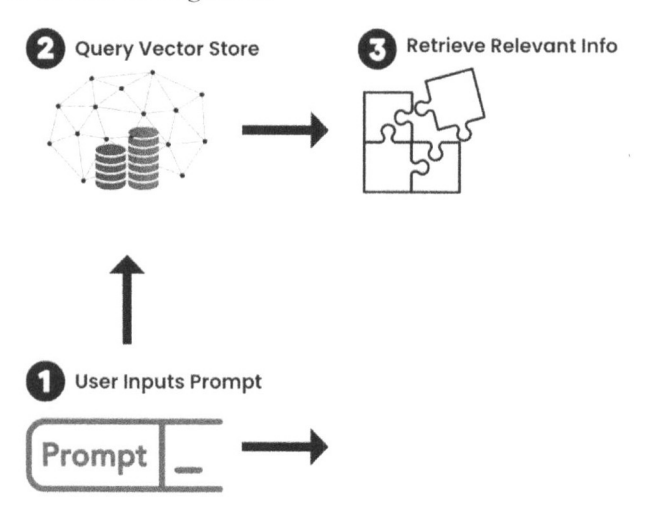

(source: https://www.freecodecamp.org/news/langchain-how-to-create-custom-knowledge-chatbots/)

After extracting the pertinent chunks that generated those vectors. we generate a completion with our LLM and subsequently produce a response (steps 4 and 5).

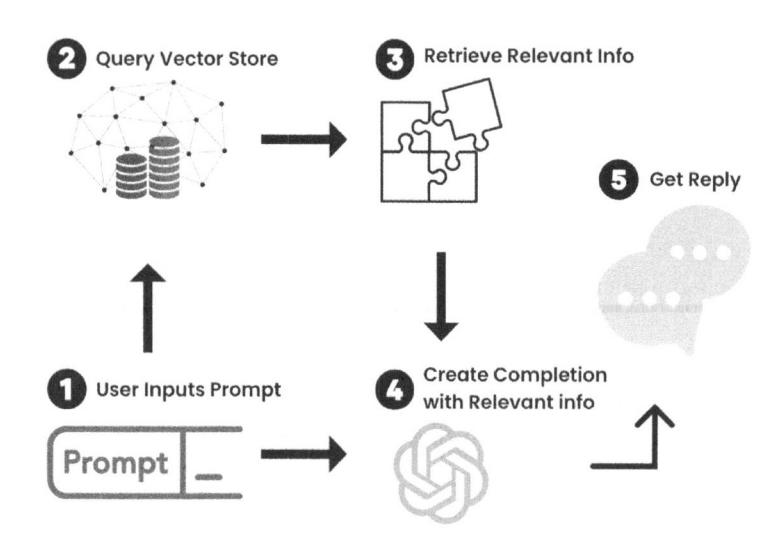

(source: https://www.freecodecamp.org/news/langchain-how-to-create-custom-knowledge-chatbots/)

In all, this turns your document into a mini Google search engine, enabling query-based searches.

Create Automated AI Workflows

Overall, LangChain can be harnessed to craft automated apps or workflows.

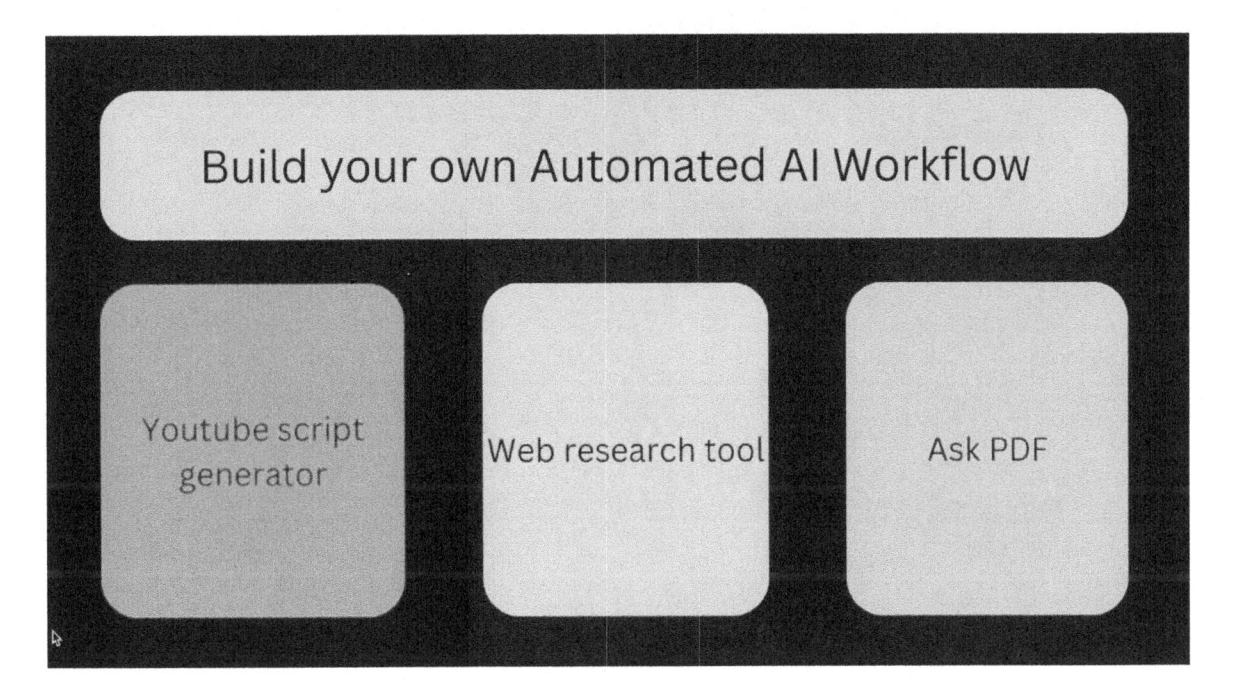

For instance, one could design a YouTube script generator or a medium article script generator (we'll build one in the next chapter). LangChain can also be employed as a web research tool, capable of summarizing voluminous texts such as documents, articles, research papers, and even books. Moreover, LangChain can be utilized to fashion question-answering systems. By inputting our documents, PDFs, or books, we can solicit answers to our queries.

Envision a scenario where one is perusing legal documents, typically necessitating a lawyer's expertise. Now, one can input a legal document or even a medical research paper into a LangChain app and pose questions to derive insights.

Chapter 4: Installation, Setup and our First LangChain App

We will now use LangChain and Streamlit to build our first app.

Medium.com is a platform where one can find stories, thoughts, articles, and expertise from writers on any subject. If your writing trends on Medium, you have the potential to amass a significant readership.

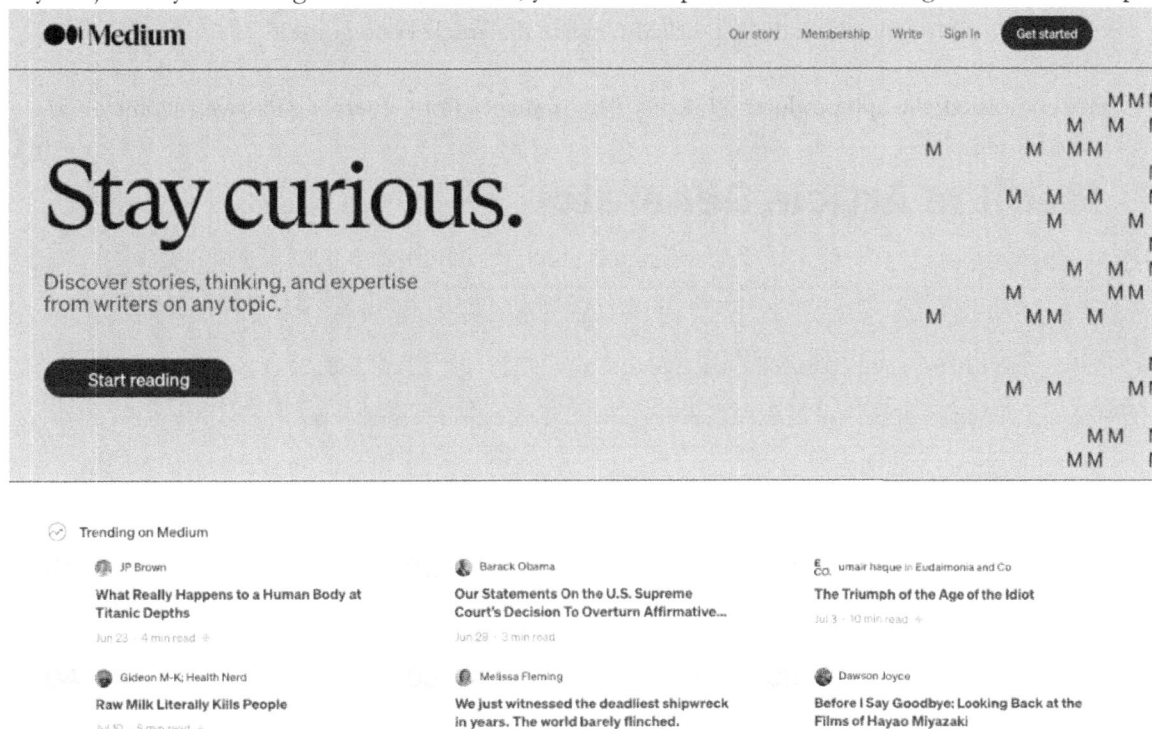

However, crafting Medium articles can be challenging. Not only does one need a captivating title, but the article's content must also be compelling.

Imagine if we had an app to assist in creating Medium articles. With the app we're developing, the goal is to design a Medium article generator that first crafts a title for us, and then, based on that title, produces an article.

The app we'll be building is a Medium article generator where you can input your topic of interest. For example, if I input "passive income" as my topic of interest and hit "enter", the app will generate a Medium title for me.

Medium Article Generator

Input your topic of interest

passive income

Following the title generation, the app will also create the article content itself.

Once completed, the app produces a title like "10 Strategies For Generating Passive Income on a Limited Budget".

Medium Article Generator

Input your topic of interest

passive income

Title: 10 Strategies For Generating Passive Income on a Limited Budget

Introduction: In today's fast-paced world, having a passive income stream has become more important than ever. It allows individuals to earn money while they sleep, creating financial stability and freedom. However, many people believe that generating passive income requires a huge upfront investment. Contrary to popular belief, there are several strategies that can be used to generate passive income on a limited budget. In this article, we will explore ten proven strategies that anyone can implement to start building a passive income portfolio, regardless of their financial situation.

1. Invest in dividend-paying stocks: Dividend-paying stocks are a great way to generate passive income, even on a limited budget. By investing in reputable companies that consistently pay dividends, individuals can enjoy regular income without needing a large capital investment.

2. Peer-to-peer lending: Utilizing peer-to-peer lending platforms allows you to earn passive income by acting as a lender. By loaning money to individuals or small businesses, you can earn interest on your investment, generating a consistent income stream.

3. Create and sell digital products: With the rise of online marketplaces, creating and selling digital products has become a popular way to earn passive income. Whether it is an e-book, online course, or stock photography, producing digital products requires minimal upfront costs but can generate steady income over time.

It also provides a subtitle, an introduction, and sections detailing various passive income streams. This output can be directly posted or edited on Medium.

Getting Started

To begin, on your computer, designate a folder to house all your LangChain-related projects. In my case, I've named it "langchain" where I store all my AI-related apps. In 'langchain', I then create a directory named "mediumarticlegenerator" and navigate to it.

```
(base) MacBook-Air-2:langchain user$ mkdir mediumarticlegenerator
(base) MacBook-Air-2:langchain user$ cd mediumarticlegenerator/
(base) MacBook-Air-2:mediumarticlegenerator user$
```

For this course, I'll be using VSCode as my Integrated Development Environment (IDE). You're welcome to use any IDE of your choice, be it PyCharm or another. In VSCode, open the "mediumarticlegenerator" folder.

Now, create a new file named "apikey.py" and another file called "app.py". In "apikey.py", define a variable named "apikey", which will store our OpenAI key.

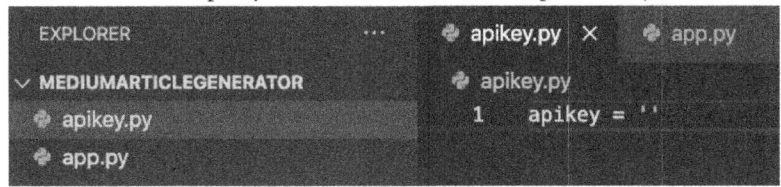

To retrieve this key, visit platform.openai.com and sign in. Under the "personal" section, you can view your API keys.

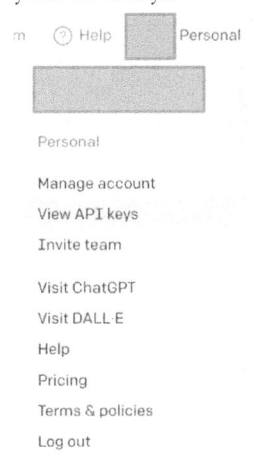

API keys

Your secret API keys are listed below. Please note that we do not display your secret API keys again after you generate them.

Do not share your API key with others, or expose it in the browser or other client-side code. In order to protect the security of your account, OpenAI may also automatically disable any API key that we've found has leaked publicly.

NAME	KEY	CREATED	LAST USED
Secret key	sk-...fZT7	30 Jun 2022	1 Sept 2022
udemy	sk-...VLV9	21 Jul 2023	21 Jul 2023

+ Create new secret key

Create a new secret key:

Create new secret key

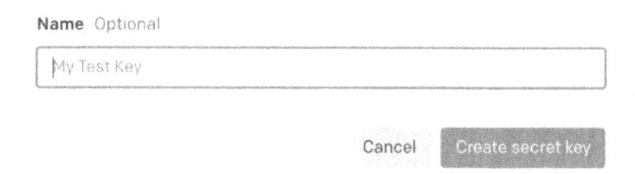

Name Optional

My Test Key

Cancel   Create secret key

Remember, always protect your API key. Sharing it or exposing it publicly could lead to unwanted charges on OpenAI.

Once you've generated your API key, return to your app and paste it in.

```
apikey = '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'
```

We'll begin by utilizing OpenAI's GPT as our LLM, and later, we'll explore other models like Hugging Face.

In "app.py", we'll first import necessary modules and set up our API key for OpenAI access. Add in the below codes into app.py:

```
import os
from apikey import apikey
os.environ["OPENAI_API_KEY"] = apikey
```

Then, we'll install several dependencies, Streamlit (for our user interface), LangChain and OpenAI. In the Terminal, run:

```
pip install streamlit langchain langchain-openai
```

* Note: Alternatively, if you want to ensure you can run the code in this book without dependency versioning issues, run:
```
pip install streamlit==1.32.2 langchain==0.1.14 langchain-openai==0.1.1
```

We will explain more on the dependencies later in the book.

After setting up the dependencies, we'll design the front end of our app using Streamlit. Add in the below codes in **bold** into app.py:

```
import os
from apikey import apikey
```

`import streamlit as st`

```
os.environ ["OPENAI_API_KEY"] = apikey
```

`st.title('Medium Article Generator')`
`topic = st.text_input('Input your topic of interest')`

This creates a title and a text input field where users can specify the topic they want an article about. We'll run our app by running in the Terminal:

```
streamlit run app.py
```

```
(base) MacBook-Air-2:mediumarticlegenerator user$ streamlit run app.py

  You can now view your Streamlit app in your browser.

  Local URL: http://localhost:8501
  Network URL: http://192.168.18.10:8501
```

It will show in the browser.

Medium Article Generator

Input your topic of interest

Currently, if users input a topic, no article will be generated since we haven't yet integrated it with OpenAI. We'll address this in the next chapter.

CHAPTER 5: CONNECTING TO OPENAI LLM

Let's proceed with connecting to OpenAI. Add in the codes in **bold**:

```
import os
from apikey import apikey

import streamlit as st
```
from langchain_openai import OpenAI

```
os.environ ["OPENAI_API_KEY"] = apikey

st.title('Medium Article Generator')
topic = st.text_input('Input your topic of interest')
```

llm = OpenAI(temperature=0.9)

Code Explanation

```
from langchain_openai import OpenAI
```

We import "OpenAI" from the LangChain LLM modules.

```
llm = OpenAI(temperature=0.9)
```

To establish a connection with OpenAI, we first instantiate an OpenAI instance. Within this constructor, we specify the temperature, which I'll set to 0.9.

You might wonder, what is this temperature parameter?

The temperature value influences the creativity of our model. A higher temperature setting results in more creativity, while a lower setting leads to more factual and objective outputs. A more factual response also tends to reduce potential inaccuracies or hallucinations from the model. The appropriate temperature setting depends on the application. For our current endeavor, which aims to generate creative article titles, a higher temperature is preferred. However, for tasks requiring factual accuracy, such as summarizing a legal document, a lower temperature might be more suitable.

With our temperature set, let's progress with our app.

Ensuring User has Entered a Topic

Before proceeding, we should ensure the user has entered a topic. Add in the **codes**:

...

...

```
llm = OpenAI(temperature=0.9)

if topic:
    response = llm.invoke(topic)
    st.write(response)
```

If a topic is provided, it will be processed by the llm and the response will be displayed in the user interface.

After saving these changes, remember to rerun the Streamlit app due to the updated source code.

i Source file changed. Rerun Always rerun ≡

To test, let's input a generic question like "Who is the fastest man alive?" As an answer, we receive "The current fastest man alive is Usain Bolt", confirming our successful connection to OpenAI.

Medium Article Generator

Input your topic of interest

Who is the fastest man alive?

Usain Bolt is widely considered to be the fastest man alive. He holds the world record for the 100m sprint at 9.58 seconds.

Another test could involve requesting a Medium article title on a topic, say, "give me a medium article title on passive income". The response might be " How to Create Multiple Streams of Passive Income and Achieve Financial Freedom".

Medium Article Generator

Input your topic of interest

give me a medium article title on passive income

"How to Create Multiple Streams of Passive Income and Achieve Financial Freedom"

Avoiding Repetitive Input

However, you'll notice that the prompt requires repetitive input, such as "Give me a Medium article title on..." followed by the topic.

Medium Article Generator

Input your topic of interest

give me a medium article title on passive income

This redundancy can be addressed using prompt templates, which we'll explore in the next chapter. With templates, we can streamline the input process, ensuring users don't have to repetitively type the same prefix for every request.

CHAPTER 6: PROMPT TEMPLATES

To avoid repetitively using "Give me a Medium article on...", we'll treat this as a prompt template. Back in our app.py, add in **bold**:

```
import os
from apikey import apikey

import streamlit as st
from langchain_openai import OpenAI
from langchain.prompts import PromptTemplate

os.environ ["OPENAI_API_KEY"] = apikey

st.title('Medium Article Generator')
topic = st.text_input('Input your topic of interest')

title_template = PromptTemplate(
  input_variables=['topic', 'language'],
  template='Give me medium article title on {topic} in {language}'
)

llm = OpenAI(temperature=0.9)

if topic:
    response = llm.invoke(topic)
    response = llm.invoke(title_template.format(topic=topic,language='english'))
    st.write(response)
```

Code Explanation

from langchain.prompts import PromptTemplate

We import the prompt template from LangChain.

```
title_template = PromptTemplate(
    input_variables=['topic', 'language'],
    template='Give me medium article title on {topic} in {language}'
)
```

Having imported the prompt template, we create a Prompt Template instance 'title_template'. This PromptTemplate will accept input variables, which we declare in an *input_variables* array. Here, we specify *topic* and *language* as input variables.

The template is a string "Give me a Medium article title on {topic} in {language}". This could translate to "Give me a Medium article title on real estate investing in Chinese", or any other language like French or German.

```
...
if topic:
    response = llm.invoke(title_template.format(topic=topic,language='english'))
```

Next, we input *title_template* to our LLM. We obtain the topic from the text input and insert it into our template (we hardcode *language* to 'english' at the moment).

Running our App

Let's save these changes and test our setup. In our app, if we input "investing", we get the title " A Beginner's Guide to Investing: How to Get Started and Maximize Your Returns".

Medium Article Generator

Input your topic of interest

investing

"A Beginner's Guide to Investing: How to Get Started and Maximize Your Returns"

```
...
if topic:
    response = llm.invoke(title_template.format(topic=topic,language='french'))
```

If I change the language to French and rerun, the title is indeed presented in French:

Input your topic of interest

investing

Comment Investir pour Garantir un Revenu Passif Régulier

The advantage of using prompt templates is evident. They offer both reusability and precision. Whether you wish to change the language or the topic, you can do so without having to repeat the initial part of the template.

Chapter 7: Simple Chains

In this chapter, we will delve into chains, beginning with a simple chain. In app.py, import LLMChain with:

```
import os
from apikey import apikey

import streamlit as st
from langchain_openai import OpenAI
from langchain.prompts import PromptTemplate
from langchain.chains import LLMChain
...
...
```

But first, why do we need chains?

While our language models can handle a plethora of tasks, they might be constrained when operating in isolation. Up to this point, we've employed LLMs for straightforward tasks: using a prompt template, feeding it to the language model, and obtaining a response. However, for more complex tasks, we'll need chains, starting with the most basic: the simple chain.

We've already imported our LLMChain. Make the code changes in the below in **bold**:

```
...
from langchain.chain import LLMChain

os.environ ["OPENAI_API_KEY"] = apikey

st.title('Medium Article Generator')
topic = st.text_input('Input your topic of interest')
language = st.text_input('Input language')

title_template = PromptTemplate(
  input_variables=['topic', 'language'],
  template='Give me medium article title on {topic} in {language}'
)

llm = OpenAI(temperature=0.9)
```

```
title_chain = LLMChain(llm=llm, prompt=title_template, verbose=True)

if topic:
    response = llm(title_template.format(topic=topic,language='english'))
    response = title_chain.invoke({'topic': topic,'language': language })
    st.write(response['text'])
```

Code Explanation

```
st.title('Medium Article Generator')
topic = st.text_input('Input your topic of interest')
language = st.text_input('Input language')
```

In our Streamlit interface, we let users specify both a topic and a language with text inputs.

```
title_chain = LLMChain(llm=llm, prompt=title_template, verbose=True)
```

After creating an OpenAI instance, we initialize our chain, which we call title_chain. This chain expects both an LLM and a prompt.

```
    response = llm(title_template.format(topic=topic,language='english'))
    response = title_chain.invoke({'topic':topic,'language':language})
```

Instead of directly invoking the LLM with our prompt template, we'll run the chain itself.
Because our title template requires two input variables, we use a dictionary. Later, I'll demonstrate how to execute this with just one input variable.

Running our App

Medium Article Generator

Input your topic of interest

aeroplane

Input language

english

"The History and Evolution of the Modern Aeroplane"

Specify a topic of interest and input language, and you will receive an article title as response.

Medium Article Generator

Input your topic of interest

aeroplane

Input language

german

"Fliegen wie ein Vogel: Alles über Aeroplanflüge"

If you observe the terminal while the program runs, you'll notice the logs detailing the chain's operations, thanks to the *verbose=True* setting:

```
title_chain = LLMChain(llm=llm, prompt=title_template, verbose=True)
```

```
> Entering new LLMChain chain...
Prompt after formatting:
Give me medium article title on aeroplane in english

> Finished chain.


> Entering new LLMChain chain...
Prompt after formatting:
Give me medium article title on aeroplane in german

> Finished chain.
```

Single Input Variable

If we simplify our input to just a single variable (removing the language parameter), the chain's execution becomes even more straightforward.

```
...
from langchain.chain import LLMChain

os.environ ["OPENAI_API_KEY"] = apikey

st.title('Medium Article Generator')
topic = st.text_input('Input your topic of interest')
language = st.text_input('Input language')

title_template = PromptTemplate(
   input_variables=['topic', 'language'],
   template='Give me medium article title on {topic} in {language}'
)

llm = OpenAI(temperature=0.9)
title_chain = LLMChain(llm=llm, prompt=title_template, verbose=True)

if topic:
   response = title_chain.invoke(topic)
   st.write(response['text'])
```

In *title_chain.invoke*, instead of a dictionary, a single string variable will suffice.

In summary, this chapter introduced simple chains, the foundational type of chain. They're easy to set up but offer limited capabilities. For complex operations, we often need to resort to sequential chains, which we'll explore in the next chapter.

CHAPTER 8: SEQUENTIAL CHAINS

So far, we have been using simple chains. We've used a title template, taken a topic, formed a string — "Give me a medium article title on {topic}" — and fed this to our chain. However, for more complex tasks, we can utilize sequential chains.

For instance, currently, we only generate a medium article title. But what if we also want the medium article content? Simple chains have their limits. In this demonstration with sequential chains, we'll first ask our model to provide a medium article title. Once we receive the title, we'll use it as an input for a second chain to obtain the article content. The process will become clearer as we proceed.

First, we'll import the sequential chain from LangChain.chains.

```
import os
from apikey import apikey

import streamlit as st
from langchain_openai import OpenAI
from langchain.prompts import PromptTemplate
from langchain.chains import LLMChain, SimpleSequentialChain
...
```

A simple sequential chain represents a sequence of chains. Each chain has a single input and output, with the output of one chain serving as the input for the next. For instance, we'll provide a topic as input, receive a title as output, and then use that title as input for the next chain, which will then generate the article body:

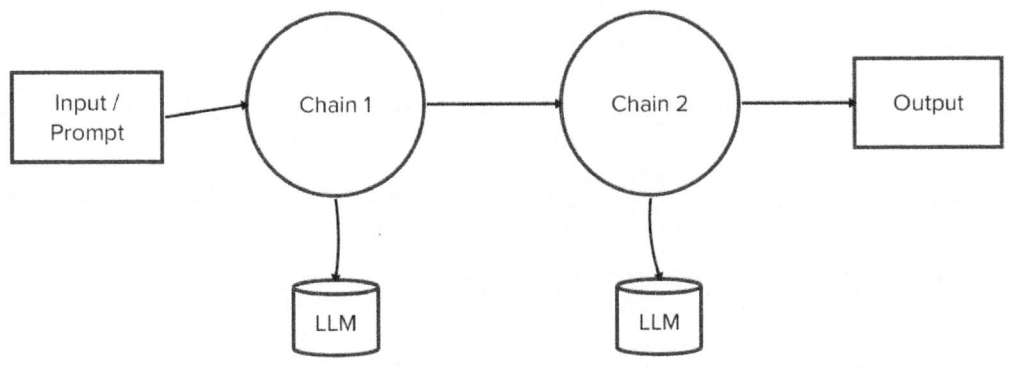

(source: https://blog.gopenai.com/zeroshot-fewshot-and-prompt-chaining-using-langchain-4259d700d67f)

Currently, we have a title template, but we'll also require a similar template for the article content. We can duplicate the title template and modify it for the article content.

```
...
from langchain.chain import LLMChain

os.environ ["OPENAI_API_KEY"] = apikey

st.title('Medium Article Generator')
topic = st.text_input('Input your topic of interest')

title_template = PromptTemplate(
    input_variables=['topic'],
    template='Give me medium article title on {topic}'
)

article_template = PromptTemplate(
    input_variables=['title'],
    template='Give me medium article for {title} including title'
)

llm = OpenAI(temperature=0.9)
title_chain = LLMChain(llm=llm, prompt=title_template, verbose=True)
article_chain = LLMChain(llm=llm, prompt=article_template, verbose=True)

if topic:
    ...
    ...
```

Code Explanation

```
article_template = PromptTemplate(
    input_variables = ['title'],
    template = 'Give me medium article for {title} including title'
)
```

This new template will take the title from the first chain as its input.

```
title_chain = LLMChain(llm=llm, prompt=title_template, verbose=True)
article_chain = LLMChain(llm=llm, prompt=article_template, verbose=True)
```

In addition to our title chain, we'll need another chain for the article content.

Flexibility of Sequential Chains

And while we're at it, let's introduce another language model to demonstrate the flexibility of sequential chains. We can use multiple models like GPT-3.5 Turbo and GPT-4. For this, we'll use the ChatOpenAI constructor, which allows us to chat with the GPT-3.5 or GPT-4 models. Add in the below in **bold**:

```
import os
from apikey import apikey

import streamlit as st
from langchain_openai import OpenAI
from langchain_openai import ChatOpenAI
from langchain.prompts import PromptTemplate
from langchain.chains import LLMChain, SimpleSequentialChain
...
...
llm = OpenAI(temperature=0.9)
title_chain = LLMChain(llm=llm, prompt=title_template, verbose=True)

llm2 = ChatOpenAI(model_name='gpt-4', temperature=0.9)
article_chain = LLMChain(llm=llm2, prompt=article_template, verbose=True)

if topic:
    ...
    ...
```

Linking Them All Together

Now, having set up two LMs, two prompt templates, and two chains, it's time to link them all together. We'll establish an overarching chain using the SimpleSequentialChain with the below code in **bold**:

```
...
...
llm = OpenAI(temperature=0.9)
title_chain = LLMChain(llm=llm, prompt=title_template, verbose=True)

llm2 = ChatOpenAI(model_name='gpt-4', temperature=0.9)
article_chain = LLMChain(llm=llm2, prompt=article_template, verbose=True)
```

```
overall_chain = SimpleSequentialChain(chains=[title_chain,
article_chain], verbose=True)

if topic:
    response = overall_chain.invoke(topic)
    st.write(response['output'])
```

We list our chains in the order they should execute. The chains will run sequentially from left to right.

After saving our changes and heading back to the browser, we can test our updated setup. For instance, when I input "running" as the topic, I receive both a title and the corresponding article content.

Medium Article Generator

Input your topic of interest

running

Title: 5 Tips to Take Your Running to the Next Level

Introduction: Running is a popular exercise that offers numerous health benefits, both physically and mentally. Whether you are just starting out or have been running for a while, there are always ways to improve and take your running to the next level. In this article, we will share five essential tips that can help you enhance your running performance and achieve your goals.

1. Set Clear and Attainable Goals: Setting clear and attainable goals is crucial to elevate your running to the next level. Determine what you want to achieve, whether it's improving your speed, increasing your endurance, or participating in a race. Break down these long-term goals into smaller, measurable milestones. This will help you stay motivated and track your progress effectively.

2. Incorporate Cross-Training: Adding cross-training exercises to your routine can greatly benefit your running. Engaging in activities like strength training, yoga, cycling, or swimming helps develop your overall fitness, balance out your muscle groups, prevent injuries, and boost your running performance. Cross-training provides a well-rounded approach to fitness and enhances your abilities as a runner.

And by checking the system log, we can see the step-by-step chain execution.

```
> Entering new LLMChain chain...
Prompt after formatting:
Give me medium article title on running

> Finished chain.


'5 Tips to Take Your Running to the Next Level'


> Entering new LLMChain chain...
Prompt after formatting:
Give me medium article for

'5 Tips to Take Your Running to the Next Level'

> Finished chain.
Title: 5 Tips to Take Your Running to the Next Level

Introduction:
Running is a popular exercise that offers numerous he
tarting out or have been running for a while, there a
In this article, we will share five essential tips th
oals.

1. Set Clear and Attainable Goals:
Setting clear and attainable goals is crucial to elev
eve, whether it's improving your speed, increasing yo
m goals into smaller, measurable milestones. This wil

2. Incorporate Cross-Training:
Adding cross-training exercises to your routine can g
raining, yoga, cycling, or swimming helps develop you
, and boost your running performance. Cross-training
ties as a runner.
```

To conclude, chains, whether simple or sequential, offer different levels of complexity depending on the task at hand. Your choice of chain will largely depend on the intricacy of the task you aim to achieve.

CHAPTER 9: AGENTS

In this section, we'll delve into agents. Create a new file in your folder and name it agents.py.

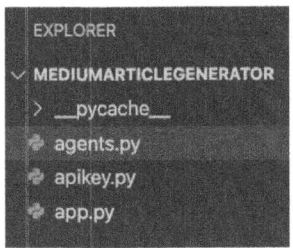

Language models are undeniably powerful. However, they sometimes struggle with tasks that even basic applications handle with ease. They might falter with logic, mathematical calculations, and communicating with external components. For instance, if you asked ChatGPT to fetch the latest article on LangChain agents, it would stumble since ChatGPT's training only extends up to September 2021. While there are plugins enabling GPT-4 to browse the internet and retrieve updated information, they are distinct from agents.

In this tutorial, we'll create a Wikipedia research tool, demonstrating agent functionality and its applications.

To begin, reconnect to OpenAI. You can reuse some code from our previous programs, such as importing the OS and API key. Additionally, you'll want to import OpenAI and several items from langchain agents. Add into agents.py:

```
import os
from apikey import apikey

from langchain import hub
from langchain_openai import OpenAI
from langchain.agents import load_tools, create_react_agent, AgentExecutor
os.environ["OPENAI_API_KEY"] = apikey

# we set temperature to 0 because we want an objective research tool without hallucinations
llm = OpenAI(temperature=0.0)
```

The primary function of agents is to leverage the GPT model to determine the subsequent action. Essentially, when faced with a problem, they outline the necessary steps to find a solution. This concept will crystallize as we proceed. Add in **bold**:

```
import os
from apikey import apikey

from langchain import hub
from langchain_openai import OpenAI
from langchain.agents import load_tools, create_react_agent, AgentExecutor
os.environ["OPENAI_API_KEY"] = apikey

llm = OpenAI(temperature=0.0)
```

tools = load_tools()
prompt = hub.pull("hwchase17/react")

Agents require access to specific tools, such as Google or Wikipedia search capabilities. By combining the GPT models with these tools, agents determine their next course of action.

Checking the documentation under Integrations, then Tools (https://python.langchain.com/docs/integrations/tools/), reveal a variety of available tools:

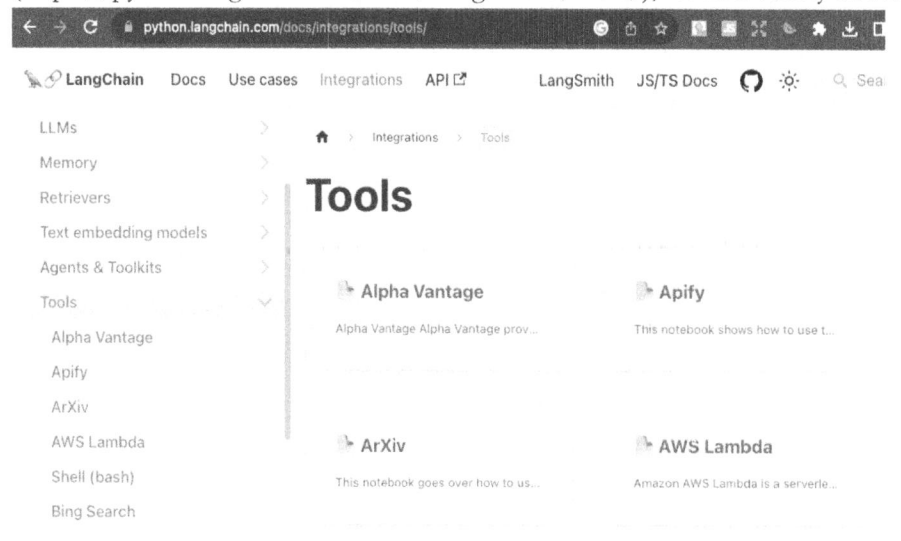

While it might be tempting to load all available tools, it's essential to equip the agent only with the necessary ones. Providing too many options may lead the agent to select an inappropriate tool, causing errors. Add the code in **bold**:

```
tools = load_tools(['wikipedia', 'llm-math'],llm)
prompt = hub.pull("hwchase17/react")
agent = create_react_agent(llm, tools, prompt)
agent_executor = AgentExecutor(agent=agent, tools=tools, verbose=True)
```

Code Explanation

```
tools = load_tools(['wikipedia', 'llm-math'],llm)
```

For this demonstration, we'll equip our agent with two tools: Wikipedia and the llm-math tool, enabling basic mathematical operations. We must also supply our language model to 'load_tools'.

```
prompt = hub.pull("hwchase17/react")
agent = create_react_agent(llm, tools, prompt)
agent_executor = AgentExecutor(agent=agent, tools=tools, verbose=True)
```

We are creating a ReAct agent by passing it the large language model, tools and the default ReAct prompt provided by LangChain. ReAct is a method that uses language models (LLMs) to think and act. It guides LLMs to come up with explanations and actions for tasks. This helps the system to think flexibly and make plans for acting, while also letting it interact with outside sources like Wikipedia to gather more information.

Each agent type serves a unique purpose, as seen from the documentation (https://python.langchain.com/docs/modules/agents/agent_types/):

Agent Types

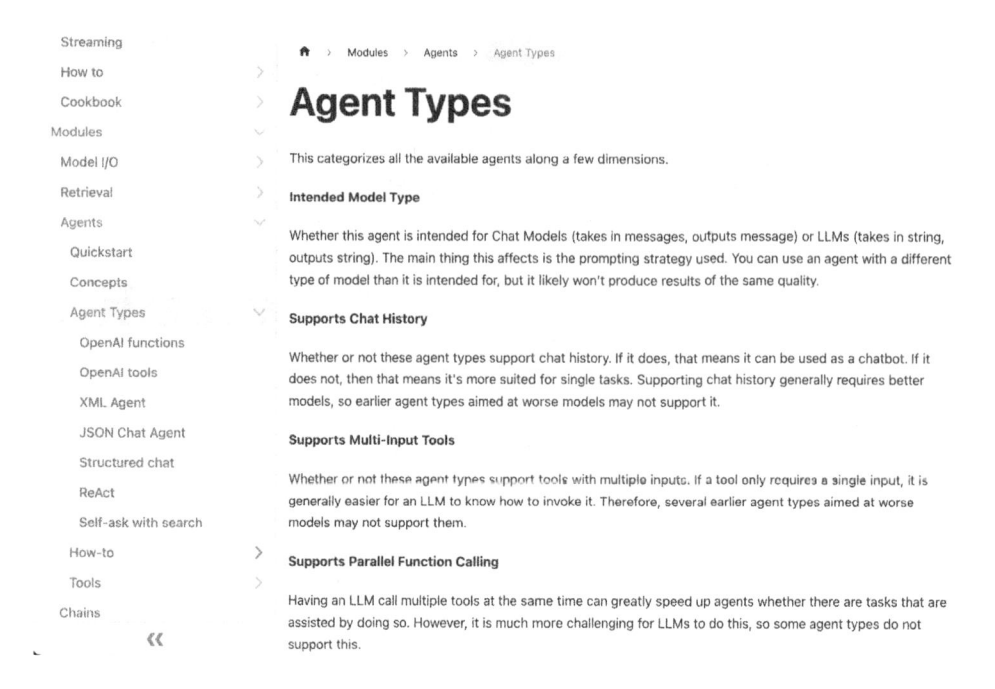

> Screenshot of LangChain docs — Agent Types page:
>
> **Agent Types**
>
> This categorizes all the available agents along a few dimensions.
>
> **Intended Model Type**
>
> Whether this agent is intended for Chat Models (takes in messages, outputs message) or LLMs (takes in string, outputs string). The main thing this affects is the prompting strategy used. You can use an agent with a different type of model than it is intended for, but it likely won't produce results of the same quality.
>
> **Supports Chat History**
>
> Whether or not these agent types support chat history. If it does, that means it can be used as a chatbot. If it does not, then that means it's more suited for single tasks. Supporting chat history generally requires better models, so earlier agent types aimed at worse models may not support it.
>
> **Supports Multi-Input Tools**
>
> Whether or not these agent types support tools with multiple inputs. If a tool only requires a single input, it is generally easier for an LLM to know how to invoke it. Therefore, several earlier agent types aimed at worse models may not support them.
>
> **Supports Parallel Function Calling**
>
> Having an LLM call multiple tools at the same time can greatly speed up agents whether there are tasks that are assisted by doing so. However, it is much more challenging for LLMs to do this, so some agent types do not support this.

For instance, a conversational or structured chat agent is optimized for interaction and may request additional inputs.

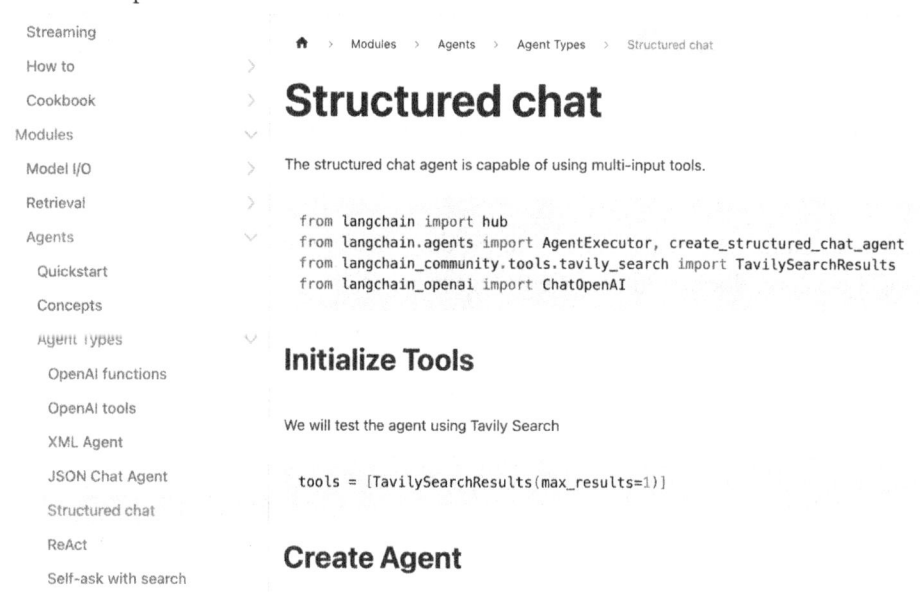

> Screenshot of LangChain docs — Structured chat page:
>
> **Structured chat**
>
> The structured chat agent is capable of using multi-input tools.
>
> ```
> from langchain import hub
> from langchain.agents import AgentExecutor, create_structured_chat_agent
> from langchain_community.tools.tavily_search import TavilySearchResults
> from langchain_openai import ChatOpenAI
> ```
>
> **Initialize Tools**
>
> We will test the agent using Tavily Search
>
> ```
> tools = [TavilySearchResults(max_results=1)]
> ```
>
> **Create Agent**

We'll employ the zero-shot react agent, the most versatile action agent:

For a deeper understanding, consult the documentation. To monitor the agent's steps, we set the verbose parameter to true, enabling a detailed log in the terminal.

Running the Agent

Although this example doesn't utilize Streamlit, it will still collect a prompt directly from the terminal. Add in **bold**:

```
...
...
prompt = hub.pull("hwchase17/react")
agent = create_react_agent(llm, tools, prompt)
agent_executor = AgentExecutor(agent=agent, tools=tools, verbose=True)

# get answer from commandline input
answer = input('Input Wikipedia Research Task\n')

agent_executor.invoke({'input': answer})
```

We feed the user input from the Terminal to the agent executor and run it using 'agent_executor.invoke'.

The agent executor evaluates it, and, based on the tools provided (ie: Wikipedia, llm-math), determines the necessary actions to solve the problem.

Running our App

Before running our app, we must install langchainhub, wikipedia and numexpr packages by running:

```
pip install langchainhub==0.1.15 wikipedia==1.4.0 numexpr==2.9.0
```

To test the setup, save the file and execute it in the terminal:

```
python agents.py
```

For a test prompt, input: "In what year did the Titanic sink?" followed by "How many years has it been since?"

```
(base) MacBook-Air-2:mediumarticlegenerator user$ python agents.py
Input Wikipedia Research Task
In what year did the Titanic sink? How many years has it been since?
```

After processing, the agent devises a plan, and as its first action: extracts information from Wikipedia:

```
> Entering new AgentExecutor chain...
 I need to find out when the Titanic sank and then calculate the difference between that year and the current
 year.
Action: Wikipedia
Action Input: Titanic
Observation: Page: Titanic
Summary: RMS Titanic was a British passenger liner, operated by the White Star Line, that sank in the North A
tlantic Ocean on 15 April 1912 after striking an iceberg during her maiden voyage from Southampton, England t
o New York City, United States. Of the estimated 2,224 passengers and crew aboard, more than 1,500 died, maki
ng it the deadliest sinking of a single ship up to that time. It remains the deadliest peacetime sinking of a
n ocean liner or cruise ship. The disaster drew public attention, provided foundational material for the disa
ster film genre, and has inspired many artistic works.
RMS Titanic was the largest ship afloat at the time she entered service and the second of three Olympic-class
 ocean liners operated by the White Star Line. She was built by the Harland and Wolff shipyard in Belfast. Th
omas Andrews, the chief naval architect of the shipyard, died in the disaster. Titanic was under the command
of Captain Edward Smith, who went down with the ship. The ocean liner carried some of the wealthiest people i
n the world, as well as hundreds of emigrants from the British Isles, Scandinavia, and elsewhere throughout E
urope, who were seeking a new life in the United States and Canada.
The first-class accommodation was designed to be the pinnacle of comfort and luxury, with a gymnasium, swimmi
ng pool, smoking rooms, high-class restaurants and cafes, a Turkish bath, and hundreds of opulent cabins. A h
igh-powered radiotelegraph transmitter was available for sending passenger "marconigrams" and for the ship's
operational use. Titanic had advanced safety features, such as watertight compartments and remotely activated
 watertight doors, contributing to its reputation as "unsinkable".
Titanic was equipped with 16 lifeboat davits, each capable of lowering three lifeboats, for a total of 48 boa
ts. However, she actually carried only 20 lifeboats, four of which were collapsible and proved hard to launch
 while she was sinking (Collapsible A nearly swamped and was filled with a foot of water until rescue; Collap
sible B completely overturned while launching). Together, the 20 lifeboats could hold 1,178 people-about half
 the number of passengers on board, and one-third of the number of passengers the ship could have carried at
full capacity (a number consistent with the maritime safety regulations of the era). When the ship sank, the
lifeboats that had been lowered were only filled up to an average of 60%.
```

It then takes the 'Calculator' action next to calculate the difference between the current year and 1912, the year the Titanic sank, delivering the answer:

```
Thought: I now know the Titanic sank in 1912.
Action: Calculator
Action Input: 2020 - 1912
Observation: Answer: 108
Thought: I now know the final answer.
Final Answer: The Titanic sank in 1912 and it has been 108 years since.
```

This example showcases the versatility and potential of agents in a myriad of applications.

CHAPTER 10: CHAT WITH A DOCUMENT

In this chapter, we'll apply what we've learned about LangChain and large language models by building a question-and-answer application for our documents.

Users can upload various file types, including PDFs, Microsoft Word documents, and text files. It then connects to the OpenAI model, and once the document is uploaded, you can begin asking questions. This "Chat with Document" chatbot app promises to be both enlightening and engaging.

Before we proceed, ensure you've installed ChromaDB. If you haven't, simply run:

```
pip install chromadb==0.4.15
```

ChromaDB is an open-source vector database. If you recall, a vector database allows applications to use vector embeddings. These embeddings convert various formats (eg. text, images, videos, audio) into numerical representations. This enables the AI to understand and attribute meaning to these representations. These numerical representations are called vectors, and vector databases are proficient at storing and querying such unstructured data, particularly during semantic searches.

In this application, we'll use the open-source vector database, ChromaDB.

For our first document, I've taken the US Constitution's text from a website and saved it as *constitution.txt* in the same directory as our Python scripts:

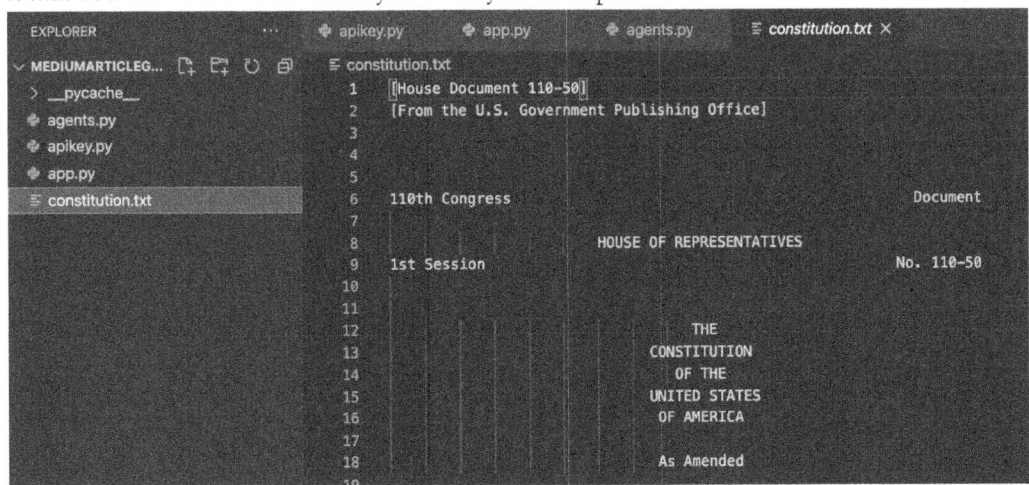

(constitution.txt is available in the source codes – contact support@i-ducate.com)

Later, we'll expand our app to allow users to upload their files, including PDFs and Word documents. But for simplicity, we'll start with this text file.

Let's create a new file named chatdoc.py. As always, we'll begin with our necessary imports and setup the OpenAI key. Add in the codes:

```
import os
from apikey import apikey
import streamlit as st # used to create our UI frontend
from langchain_openai import ChatOpenAI # used for GPT3.5/4 model
from langchain_community.document_loaders import TextLoader
from langchain.text_splitter import RecursiveCharacterTextSplitter
from langchain_openai import OpenAIEmbeddings
from langchain_community.vectorstores import Chroma
from langchain.chains import RetrievalQA

os.environ["OPENAI_API_KEY"] = apikey
st.title('Chat with Document') # title in our web page
loader = TextLoader('./constitution.txt') # to load text document
documents = loader.load()
print(documents) # print to ensure document loaded correctly.
```

(alternatively, if you don't want to copy the code, contact support@i-ducate.com for the source codes)

Run in the Terminal:

```
streamlit run chatdoc.py
```

You can see the StreamLit UI running in the browser and in the Terminal, it loads and prints the text file:

```
himself. No person shall,         5       .......  ......\n in a criminal ca
se, be compelled to be a.\n [Amendments]...........................\nWitne
sses against him. In all criminal         6        .......  ......\n prosec
utions the accused shall be\n confronted with the. [Amendments]........\nWit
nesses in his favor. In all criminal         6       .......  ......\n pros
ecutions the accused shall have\n compulsory process for obtaining.\n [Amend
ments]...........................\nWitnesses to the same overt act, or on
          3       3       1\n confession in open court. No person shal
l\n be convicted of treason unless on the\n testimony of two...............
........\nWrit of habeas corpus shall not be          1       9
      2\n suspended unless in case of rebellion or\n invasion the public saf
ety may require it\nWrits of election to fill vacancies in the          1
      2       4\n representation of any State. The\n executives of the Stat
e shall issue......\nWritten opinion of the principal officer         2
      2       1\n in each of the Executive Departments on\n any subject re
lating to the duties of his\n office. The President may require the....\n\n\n
                 Y\n\nYeas and nays of the members of either
   1       5       3\n House shall, at the desire of one-fifth\n of those p
resent, be entered on the\n journals............................\n       T
he votes of both Houses upon the          1       7       2\n        re
consideration of a bill returned by\n    the President with his objections\
n     shall be determined by..............\n-------------------------------
------------------------------------\n\n\n
    \n\x1a", metadata={'source': './constitution.txt'})]
```

Next, we have to split our document into chunks because if the text is too long, it cannot be loaded into model. We use RecursiveCharacterTextSplitter to break our text into smaller, semantically related chunks (means sentences in each chunk are semantically related to each other). Add the codes in **bold**:

```
...
...
os.environ["OPENAI_API_KEY"] = apikey
st.title('Chat with Document')
loader = TextLoader('./constitution.txt')
documents = loader.load()

text_splitter = RecursiveCharacterTextSplitter(chunk_size=1000,
chunk_overlap=200)

chunks = text_splitter.split_documents(documents)

# to see the chunks
st.write(chunks[0])
st.write(chunks[1])
```

Code Explanation

```
text_splitter = RecursiveCharacterTextSplitter(chunk_size=1000,
chunk_overlap=200)
chunks = text_splitter.split_documents(documents)
```

`RecursiveCharacterTextSplitter` is the recommended one for generic text. It tries to split the text until the chunks are small enough. Splitting text uses a default separator list of ["\n\n", "\n", " ", ""]. This has the effect of trying to keep all paragraphs (and then sentences, and then words) together as long as possible, as those would generically seem to be the strongest semantically related pieces of text.

We use the default values of 1000 for chunk size and 200 for chunk overlap. If chunk size is too small or too large, it leads to imprecise search results or missed opportunities to surface relevant content. As a rule of thumb, if a chunk makes sense to a human (without its surrounding context), it will make sense to a language model too. So, finding the optimal chunk size is quite crucial to ensure search results are accurate and relevant. You can play around with the chunk size.

Chunk overlap is the overlap between chunks you need to maintain continuity between one chunk and the next. We will see this concretely later when we run our app.

```
st.write(chunks[0])
st.write(chunks[1])
```

We print the first two individual chunks to see how they look like.

Running our App

Chat with Document

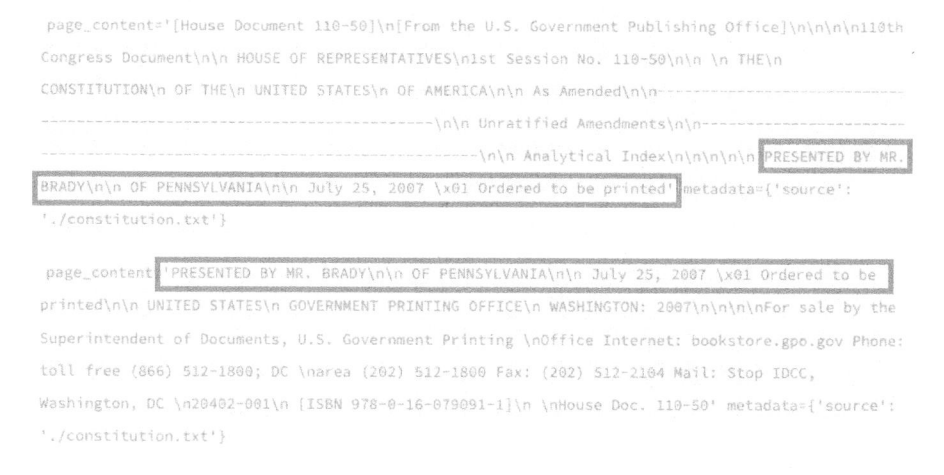

page_content='[House Document 110-50]\n[From the U.S. Government Publishing Office]\n\n\n\n110th Congress Document\n\n HOUSE OF REPRESENTATIVES\n1st Session No. 110-50\n\n \n THE\n CONSTITUTION\n OF THE\n UNITED STATES\n OF AMERICA\n\n As Amended\n\n--\n\n Unratified Amendments\n\n--\n\n Analytical Index\n\n\n\n PRESENTED BY MR. BRADY\n\n OF PENNSYLVANIA\n\n July 25, 2007 \x01 Ordered to be printed' metadata={'source': './constitution.txt'}

page_content='PRESENTED BY MR. BRADY\n\n OF PENNSYLVANIA\n\n July 25, 2007 \x01 Ordered to be printed\n\n UNITED STATES\n GOVERNMENT PRINTING OFFICE\n WASHINGTON: 2007\n\n\n\nFor sale by the Superintendent of Documents, U.S. Government Printing \nOffice Internet: bookstore.gpo.gov Phone: toll free (866) 512-1800; DC \narea (202) 512-1800 Fax: (202) 512-2104 Mail: Stop IDCC, Washington, DC \n20402-0001\n [ISBN 978-0-16-079091-1]\n \nHouse Doc. 110-50' metadata={'source': './constitution.txt'}

You can see the above two chunks. The size of each chunk is 1,000. You can also see the chunk overlap. Eg. 'PRESENTED BY MR. BRADY\n\n OF PENNSYLVANIA\n\n July 25, 2007 \x01 Ordered to be printed'.

The chunk overlap is like a rolling window across paragraphs in case there's a relevant sentence that had to be a part of the first and later chunk.

Embeddings

Once we have our chunks ready, we'll create our embeddings using OpenAI's extensive library of embeddings which is built from the corpus of text from all over the Internet.

Embeddings measure the relatedness of text strings and are commonly used for searching and clustering. Each embedding is a vector of floating point numbers where the distance between two vectors measures their relatedness.

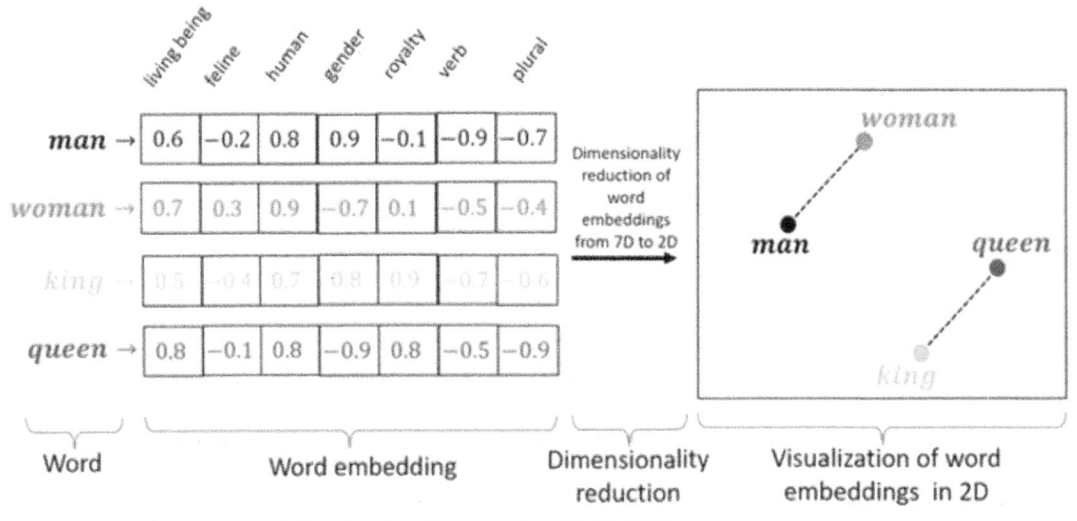

	living being	feline	human	gender	royalty	verb	plural
man →	0.6	−0.2	0.8	0.9	−0.1	−0.9	−0.7
woman →	0.7	0.3	0.9	−0.7	0.1	−0.5	−0.4
king →	0.5	−0.4	0.7	0.8	0.9	−0.7	−0.6
queen →	0.8	−0.1	0.8	−0.9	0.8	−0.5	−0.9

Dimensionality reduction of word embeddings from 7D to 2D

Word | Word embedding | Dimensionality reduction | Visualization of word embeddings in 2D

(source: https://medium.com/@hari4om/word-embedding-d816f643140)

Take for example in the above figure, 'man', 'woman', 'king', 'queen' is represented in a vector form across multiple factors ('living being', 'human', 'royalty' etc). Here, we just have seven factors but it can be 4,000-5,000. In vector form, it will seem that man and woman are closer related whereas king and queen are closer.

The idea behind embeddings is to map words or sentences to vectors. Then, these vectors are stored in a database. New sentences can be compared to these embeddings to determine their relatedness. With the embeddings in place, we'll initialize our vector database. Add in the codes in **bold**:

```
os.environ["OPENAI_API_KEY"] = apikey
st.title('Chat with Document')
loader = TextLoader('./constitution.txt')
documents = loader.load()

text_splitter = RecursiveCharacterTextSplitter(chunk_size=1000, chunk_overlap=200)

chunks = text_splitter.split_documents(documents)
embeddings = OpenAIEmbeddings()
vector_store = Chroma.from_documents(chunks, embeddings)
```

We initialize the vector store from Chroma. Chroma is an open source lightweight embeddings database that stores embeddings locally. We pass in the document chunks and the OpenAI embeddings.

Now, we can query this vector store using our retrieval chain. Add in the following in **bold**:

```
...
text_splitter = RecursiveCharacterTextSplitter(chunk_size=1000, chunk_overlap=200)

chunks = text_splitter.split_documents(documents)
embeddings = OpenAIEmbeddings()
vector_store = Chroma.from_documents(chunks, embeddings)

# initialize OpenAI instance
llm = ChatOpenAI(model='gpt-3.5-turbo', temperature=0)
retriever=vector_store.as_retriever()
chain = RetrievalQA.from_chain_type(llm, retriever=retriever)
# get question from user input
question = st.text_input('Input your question')

if question:
    # run chain
    response = chain.invoke(question)
    st.write(response['result'])
```

We tell the RetrievalQA chain, use the vector store and perform a Question and Answer retrieval. The RetrievalQA chain then look up the relevant vectors from the vector database and then ask the chain to return a response based on the user's question.

Running our App

To demonstrate, let's run our app and pose a question to the US Constitution. For instance, "What is the age requirement to be a senator?".

Chat with Document

Input your question

What is the age requirement to be a senator?

The age requirement to be a senator is 30 years old.

Our app should return "30 years" as the answer. We can ask another question:

Chat with Document

Input your question

Who can veto decisions made by the senate

The President can veto decisions made by the Senate.

Behind the scenes, the question is used to retrieve relevant documents from the vector database. It identifies pertinent documents with high similarity to keywords in the question. Once these documents are fetched, they're used, along with the model, to generate a response.

In subsequent lessons, we'll extend this application to handle PDFs and Word documents, showcasing its potential in fields like law and finance. For example, we load legal documents or financial statements, create chunks from them, embed them into a vector store, and query the documents and get the response using large language models.

Chapter 11: Adding Memory (Chat History)

Currently, we can pose a question to our document and receive a response.

We have previously received a response that a senator must be at least 30 years old. However, if I were to ask a subsequent question, like multiply that number by two, what would happen? In normal human interactions, we would understand "that" refers to 30 years old. Therefore, 30 times two is 60.

Yet, when we test this, we get a 'I don't know' response.

Chat with Document

Input your question

> multiply that by 2

I'm sorry, but I don't have enough information to answer your question. Could you please provide more context or clarify what you would like me to do with the given pieces of information?

It seems the app only considers the immediate question without acknowledging previous context. It fails to recognize follow-up questions within the scope of a larger conversation.

How can we address this?

Our app needs to remember prior questions and answers, essentially requiring a chat history. In this chapter, we'll discuss how to preserve context and add memory to our application.

Firstly, we'll transition from using the RetrievalQA to the Conversational Retrieval Chain. To implement this, make the changes in **bold**:

```
...
import streamlit as st
from langchain_openai import ChatOpenAI
from langchain_community.document_loaders import TextLoader
from langchain.text_splitter import RecursiveCharacterTextSplitter
from langchain_openai import OpenAIEmbeddings
from langchain_community.vectorstores import Chroma
from langchain.chains import RetrievalQA
from langchain.chains import ConversationalRetrievalChain
...
...
...


llm = ChatOpenAI(model='gpt-3.5-turbo', temperature=0)
retriever=vector_store.as_retriever()
chain = RetrievalQA.from_chain_type(llm, retriever=retriever)
crc = ConversationalRetrievalChain.from_llm(llm, retriever)

question = st.text_input('Input your question')

if question:
    ...
```

The conversational retrieval chain retains chat history while still leveraging retrieval capabilities.

Running the Chain with Chat History

Change the codes in **bold**:

```
...
if question:
    response = crc.invoke({'question':question,'chat_history':})
    st.write(response)
```

When you run the chain, we need to supply a dictionary that specifies the question and the chat history. To establish a chat history, we store each question and its answer in the session state. Add the codes in **bold**:

```
question = st.text_input('Input your question' )

if question:
    if 'history' not in st.session_state:
        st.session_state['history'] = []

    response = crc.invoke({
      'question':question,
      'chat_history': st.session_state['history']
    })

    st.session_state['history'].append((question, response['answer']))
    st.write(response['answer'])
```

Streamlit offers a *session_state* property, where we can store variables in a session. If *history* doesn't already exist in the session state, initialize it as an empty array. Then, append each question-response pair to this array.

Running our App

Once you've made these modifications, launch the application in Streamlit.

Now, when you ask the age requirement for senators and follow with a multiplication query, the system comprehends the entire conversation, returning a coherent response.

> Input your question
>
> what's the age to be a senator
>
> The age requirement to be a Senator is 30 years old.
>
> Input your question
>
> multiply that by 2
>
> The result of multiplying the age requirement to be a Senator by 2 is 60.

Maintaining context through chat history can significantly enhance conversational interactions. In case you got lost at any stage, here's the entire code of chatdoc.py:

```python
import os
from apikey import apikey
import streamlit as st # used to create our UI frontend
from langchain_openai import ChatOpenAI # used for GPT3.5/4 model
from langchain_community.document_loaders import TextLoader
from langchain.text_splitter import RecursiveCharacterTextSplitter
from langchain_openai import OpenAIEmbeddings
from langchain_community.vectorstores import Chroma
from langchain.chains import ConversationalRetrievalChain

os.environ["OPENAI_API_KEY"] = apikey
st.title('Chat with Document') # title in our web page
loader = TextLoader('./constitution.txt') # to load text document
documents = loader.load()

text_splitter = RecursiveCharacterTextSplitter(chunk_size=1000,
chunk_overlap=200)
chunks = text_splitter.split_documents(documents)
embeddings = OpenAIEmbeddings()
vector_store = Chroma.from_documents(chunks, embeddings)

# initialize OpenAI instance
llm = ChatOpenAI(model='gpt-3.5-turbo', temperature=0)
retriever=vector_store.as_retriever()

crc = ConversationalRetrievalChain.from_llm(llm, retriever)
# get question from user input
question = st.text_input('Input your question')

if question:
    if 'history' not in st.session_state:
        st.session_state['history'] = []

    response = crc.invoke({
        'question':question,
        'chat_history': st.session_state['history']
    })

    st.session_state['history'].append((question,response['answer']))
    st.write(response['answer'])
```

Chapter 12: Outputting Chat History

Suppose you wish to display the chat history. It's quite simple. Add the below codes in **bold**:

```
...
...
question = st.text_input('Input your question')

if question:
    if 'history' not in st.session_state:
        st.session_state['history'] = []

    response = crc.invoke({
     'question':question,
     'chat_history': st.session_state['history']
    })

    st.session_state ['history'].append((question, response['answer']))
    st.write(response['answer'])
    st.write(st.session_state['history'])
```

After saving your changes and rerunning the program, you'll observe the chat history displayed.

Chat with Document

Input your question

multiply that by 2

The result of multiplying the age requirement to be a Senator by 2 is 60.

```
▼ [
   ▼ 0 : [
       0 : "what's the age to be a senator"
       1 : "The age requirement to be a Senator is 30 years old."
     ]
   ▼ 1 : [
       0 : "multiply that by 2"
       1 :
       "The result of multiplying the age requirement to be a Senator by 2 is 60."
     ]
 ]
```

The chat history appears to be structured like a 2D array.

For a more structured printout, consider using a *for* loop. Add the codes in **bold** to iterate through each entry in the session state.

```
if question:
    if 'history' not in st.session_state:
        st.session_state['history'] = []

    response = crc.invoke({
     'question':question,
     'chat_history': st.session_state ['history']
    })

    st.session_state ['history' ].append((question, response['answer']))
    st.write(response['answer'])
    st.write(st.session_state['history'])
    for prompts in st.session_state ['history']:
      st.write("Question: " + prompts[0])
      st.write("Answer: " + prompts[1])
```

For each entry, the first index corresponds to the question, and the second index represents the answer. By implementing this, the output will be more organized and easier to interpret.

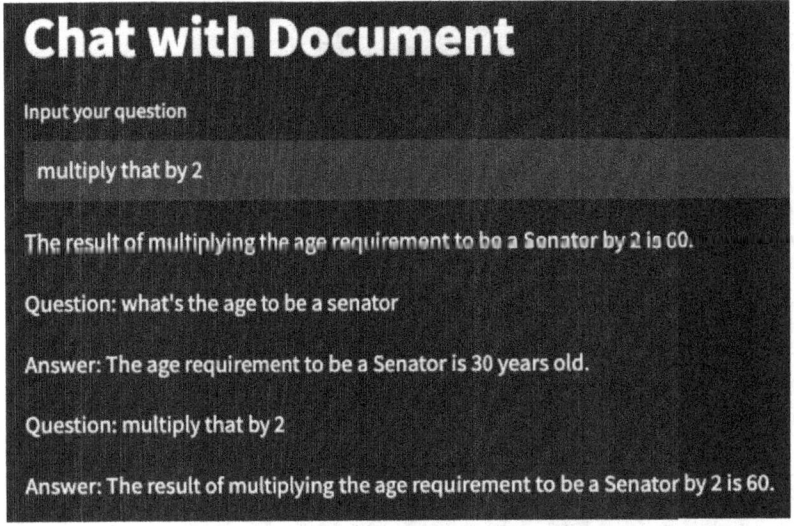

Chat with Document

Input your question

multiply that by 2

The result of multiplying the age requirement to be a Senator by 2 is 60.

Question: what's the age to be a senator

Answer: The age requirement to be a Senator is 30 years old.

Question: multiply that by 2

Answer: The result of multiplying the age requirement to be a Senator by 2 is 60.

However, we now face an issue. The chat history persists indefinitely, leading to an ever-growing chat log. Another issue is that users are limited to the Constitution text. How should we allow users to upload different files, like PDFs or Word documents, and also refresh the chat history? We'll delve into these aspects in the next chapter.

Chapter 13: Uploading Custom Documents

In this chapter, we let users upload their own documents. Add in the following codes in **bold**:

```
...
...
from Langchain.chains import ConversationalRetrievalChain

os.environ ["OPENAI_API_KEY"] = apikey

def clear_history():
    if 'history' in st.session_state:
        del st.session_state['history']

st.title( 'Chat with Document')
uploaded_file = st.file_uploader('Upload file:', type=['pdf','docx','txt'])
add_file = st.button('Add File', on_click=clear_history)
loader = TextLoader ('./constitution.txt')

documents = loader.load()
...
...
```

Code Explanation

```
...
st.title( 'Chat with Document')
uploaded_file = st.file_uploader('Upload file:',type=['pdf','docx','txt'])
```

We include a file uploader with the message "Upload file." We specify that we accept file types like PDF, DOCX, and TXT. Once the file is uploaded, it will be stored in the *uploaded_file* variable.

```
uploaded_file = st.file_uploader('Upload file:', type=['pdf','docx','txt'))
add_file = st.button('Add File', on_click=clear_history)
```

Following the file upload, we have a button with the label "Add file." This button will be activated by the user when they're ready to upload their chosen document. The *on_click* event will trigger the *clear_history* method when the button is clicked.

```python
def clear_history():
    if 'history' in st.session_state:
        del st.session_state['history']
```

The *clear_history* method ensures that each time we upload a new document, the previous chat history is cleared.

Uploading and Reading the File

To read the file, add the codes in **bold**:

```
...
...
add_file = st.button( 'Add File', on_click=clear_history)

if uploaded_file and add_file:
    bytes_data = uploaded_file.read()
    file_name = os.path. join('./', uploaded_file.name)
    with open (file_name, 'wb') as f:
        f.write(bytes_data)

    loader = TextLoader(file_name)
    documents = loader.load()
...
...
```

Code Explanation

```
if uploaded_file and add_file:
```

This check ensures that the program only progresses with the file upload once the file has been specified and the "Add file" button has been clicked. Without this check, the program might mistakenly attempt to upload a non-existent file, resulting in errors.

```
    bytes_data = uploaded_file.read()
```

Once the file is uploaded, its content will be read in binary format and stored in the *bytes_data* variable.

```
file_name = os.path.join('./', uploaded_file.name)
```

The binary data will then be copied into a file in the current directory, retaining the same name as the uploaded file. You can choose to save this to any directory by specifying the desired path. This action will return the file name.

```
with open (file_name, 'wb') as f:
    f.write(bytes_data)
```

Next, the program will open the file in binary read mode.

```
loader = TextLoader(file_name)
```

Finally in TextLoader, replace the hardcoding of constitution.txt with *file_name*.

Processing the File

At this point, the file name is supplied to our text loader. Ensure proper indentation to maintain the correct scope:

```
if uploaded_file and add_file:
   bytes_data = uploaded_file.read()
   file_name = os.path.join('./', uploaded_file.name)
   with open(file_name, 'wb') as f:
      f.write(bytes_data)

   # move code under 'if' scope
   loader = TextLoader(file_name)
   documents = loader.load()

   text_splitter = RecursiveCharacterTextSplitter (...)
   ...
   ...

   crc = ConversationalRetrievalChain.from_llm(llm, retriever)
```

```
question = st.text_input('Input your question')

if question:
    ...
    ...
```

If you run your code now, you get an error:

Input your question

what's the age to be a senator

NameError: name 'crc' is not defined

Traceback:

File "/Users/user/anaconda3/lib/python3.10/site-packages/streamlit/runtime/scr
    exec(code, module.__dict__)
File "/Users/user/Documents/langchain/mediumarticlegenerator/chatdoc.py", line
    response = crc.run({

This is because *crc*, the `ConversationalRetrievalChain` instance, is now in a different scope with the below:

```
    ...
    crc = ConversationalRetrievalChain.from_llm(llm, retriever)

question = st.text_input('Input your question')

if question:
    if 'history' not in st.session_state:
        st.session_state['history'] = []

    response = crc.invoke({
        'question':question,
        'chat_history': st.session_state['history']
    })
    ...
```

We thus store *crc* in the session state for it to be accessible to all. Add the following in **bold**:

```
...

...

crc = ConversationalRetrievalChain.from_llm(llm, retriever)

st.session_state.crc = crc

# success message when file is chunked & embedded successfully
st.success('File uploaded, chunked and embedded successfully')

question = st.text_input('Input your question')

if question:
    if 'crc' in st.session_state:
        crc = st.session_state.crc

        # indent below code to make sure scope is correct
        if 'history' not in st.session_state:
            st.session_state['history'] = []

        ...

        ...
        for prompts in st.session_state ['history']:
            st.write("Question: " + prompts[0])
            st.write("Answer: " + prompts[1])
```

Thus, the entire process—chunking, embedding, etc.—will only proceed if a file has been uploaded and the "Add file" button clicked. This avoids unnecessary expenses tied to processing.

Now, let's save our progress and rerun the program. Browse and select the constitution.txt (or your own file) and click "Add file"

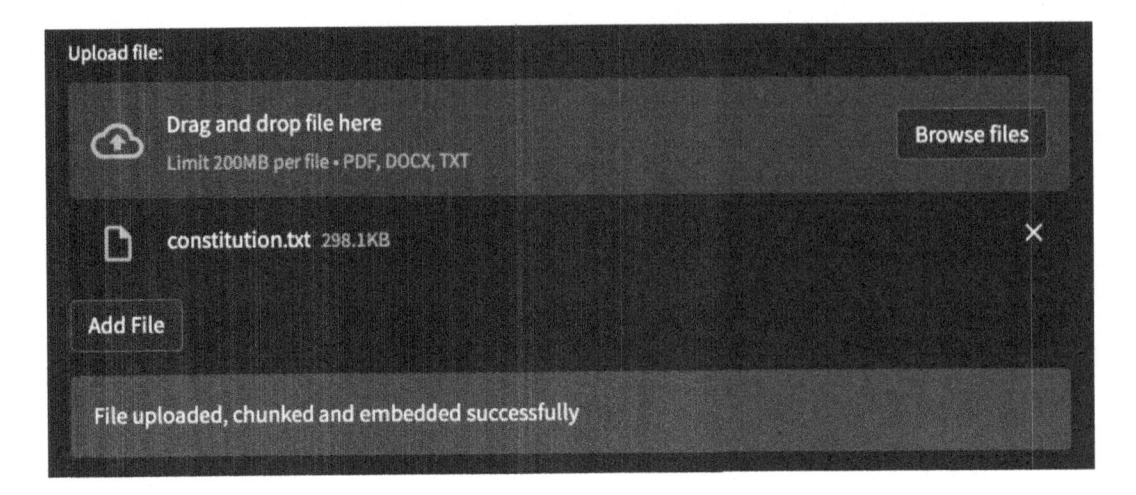

We can then ask a question, such as the age requirement to become a senator.

If everything runs smoothly, the chat history should display the correct responses.

When a new file is uploaded, the chat history resets. Because of the codes:

```
def clear_history():
   if 'history' in st.session_state:
      del st.session_state['history']

...
add_file = st.button ('Add File', on_click=clear_history)
```

This ensures that the program remains contextually accurate.

In conclusion, we've successfully added a file upload feature and the capability to refresh the chat history. In the following chapter, we'll extend the file uploading feature to accommodate more file types, including PDF and Word files.

In case you get lost at any point, here's the entire code of chatdoc.py:

```python
import os
from apikey import apikey
import streamlit as st # used to create our UI frontend
from langchain_openai import ChatOpenAI # used for GPT3.5/4 model
from langchain_community.document_loaders import TextLoader
from langchain.text_splitter import RecursiveCharacterTextSplitter
from langchain_openai import OpenAIEmbeddings
from langchain_community.vectorstores import Chroma
from langchain.chains import ConversationalRetrievalChain

os.environ["OPENAI_API_KEY"] = apikey

def clear_history():
    if 'history' in st.session_state:
        del st.session_state['history']

st.title('Chat with Document') # title in our web page

uploaded_file = st.file_uploader('Upload file:',type=['pdf','docx','txt'])
add_file = st.button('Add File', on_click=clear_history)

if uploaded_file and add_file:
    bytes_data = uploaded_file.read()
    file_name = os.path.join('./', uploaded_file.name)
    with open (file_name, 'wb') as f:
        f.write(bytes_data)

    loader = TextLoader(file_name)
    documents = loader.load()

    text_splitter = RecursiveCharacterTextSplitter(chunk_size=1000,
```

```python
        chunk_overlap=200)
        chunks = text_splitter.split_documents(documents)
        embeddings = OpenAIEmbeddings()
        vector_store = Chroma.from_documents(chunks, embeddings)

        # initialize OpenAI instance
        llm = ChatOpenAI(model='gpt-3.5-turbo', temperature=0)
        retriever=vector_store.as_retriever()

        crc = ConversationalRetrievalChain.from_llm(llm, retriever)

        st.session_state.crc = crc

        # success message when file is chunked & embedded successfully
        st.success('File uploaded, chunked and embedded successfully')

# get question from user input
question = st.text_input('Input your question')

if question:
    if 'crc' in st.session_state:
        crc = st.session_state.crc

        if 'history' not in st.session_state:
            st.session_state['history'] = []

        response = crc.invoke({
            'question':question,
            'chat_history': st.session_state['history']
        })

        st.session_state['history'].append((question,response['answer']))
        st.write(response['answer'])
        for prompts in st.session_state ['history']:
            st.write("Question: " + prompts[0])
            st.write("Answer: " + prompts[1])
```

CHAPTER 14: LOADING DIFFERENT FILE TYPES

We'll explore how to load different file formats, such as text files, PDFs, and Word documents, into our LangChain app.
Before the code changes, we will need pypdf and docx2txt libraries to parse and extract text from these document types. Run the below to install the same.

```
pip install pypdf==4.1.0 docx2txt==0.8
```

Currently, we only accept text files, which we load via the text loader. What we'll do is examine the file extension—be it .txt, .pdf, or .doc—and use the appropriate loader based on that. Add the codes in **bold**:
...
...
```
if uploaded_file and add_file:
    with st.spinner('Reading, chunking and embedding file...'):
        bytes_data = uploaded_file.read()
        file_name = os.path.join('./', uploaded_file.name)
        with open(file_name,'wb') as f:
            f.write(bytes_data)

        name, extension = os.path.splitext(file_name)

        if extension == '.pdf':
            from langchain_community.document_loaders import PyPDFLoader
            loader = PyPDFLoader(file_name)
        elif extension == '.docx':
            from langchain_community.document_loaders import Docx2txtLoader
            loader = Docx2txtLoader(file_name)
        elif extension == '.txt':
            from langchain_community.document_loaders import TextLoader
            loader = TextLoader(file_name)
        else:
            st.write('Document format is not supported!')

        documents = loader.load()
```
...
...

Code Explanation

```
name, extension = os.path.splitext(file_name)
```

To extract the file extension, we utilize the *os.path.splitext()* method, where we input the filename and receive both the filename and its extension in return.

```
if extension == '.pdf':
    from langchain.document_loaders import PyPDFLoader
    loader = PyPDFLoader(file_name)
```

Based on the extension, we'll choose the corresponding loader. If the extension is .pdf, we'll import the PyPDFLoader, which aids in loading PDFs. Following that, we'll use *loader = PyPDFLoader* and provide the filename.

```
elif extension == '.docx':
    from langchain.document_loaders import Docx2txtLoader
    loader = Docx2txtLoader(file_name)
```

If the extension is a .docx, we'll utilize the `Docx2txtLoader`.

```
...
import streamlit as st
from langchain. chat_models import ChatOpenAI
from langchain. document_loaders import TextLoader
from langchain. text_splitter import RecursiveCharacterTextSplitter
...
...
    elif extension == '.txt':
        from langchain.document_loaders import TextLoader
        loader = TextLoader(file_name)
```

For a .txt extension, we'll use our existing *TextLoader*. We also relocate the import statements here so that we don't inadvertently import the textLoader when it's not in use.

```
else:
    st.write('Document format is not supported!')

documents = loader.load()
```

There might be scenarios where a user uploads a file with an extension we don't currently support. In such cases, a notification or alert could be beneficial.

After loading, the rest of the process remains unchanged, regardless of the file type. It's just the source that varies based on the file extension.

If you're curious about adding support for a new file type or extension and need the appropriate loader, you can consult the LangChain documentation. Here, you'll find a range of integrations they offer. For instance, if you're looking for a Powerpoint integration, it will guide you to use the *UnstructuredPowerPointLoader*.

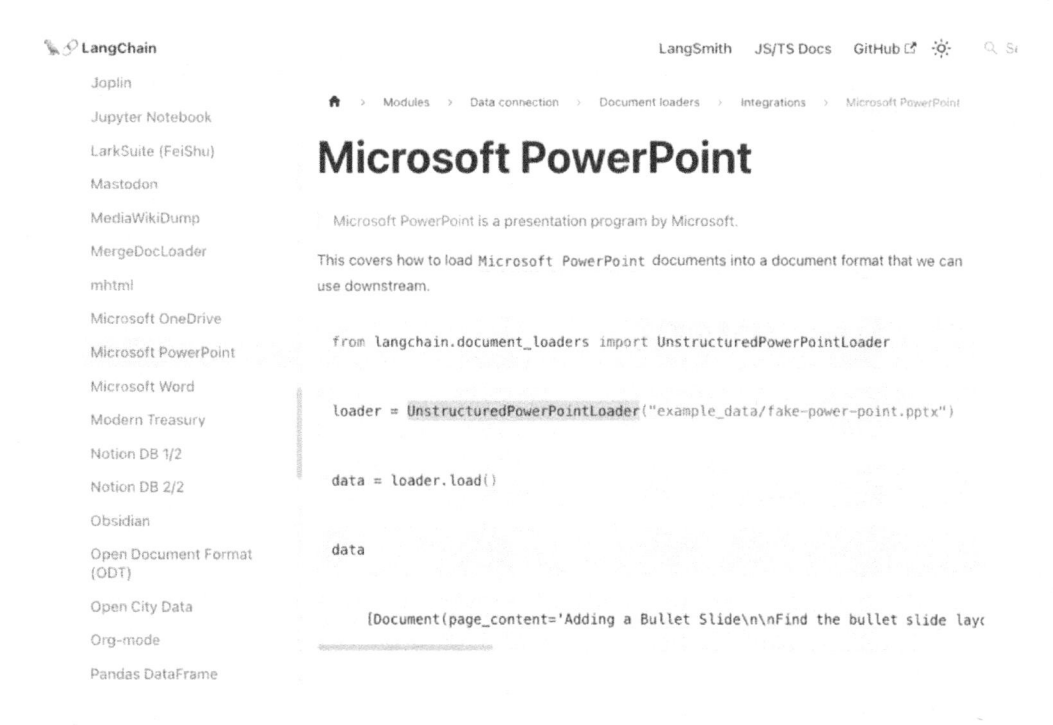

Displaying a Spinner While Waiting

Currently, when a user uploads a file, there's a perceivable wait time during the chunking and embedding phases. By adding a spinner with a message like "Reading, Chunking, and Embedding File", users will have a visual cue that processing is in progress. Add in **bold**:

...

```
...
if uploaded_file and add_file:
    with st.spinner('Reading, chunking and embedding file...'):
        bytes_data = uploaded_file.read()
        file_name = os.path.join('./', uploaded_file.name)
        with open(file_name,'wb') as f:
            f.write(bytes_data)
        ...
        ...
        st.session_state.crc = crc
        st.success('File uploaded, chunked and embedded successfully')

question = st.text_input('Input your question')
```

Ensure you indent the rest of the code under the spinner's scope.

Running Our App

Let's test our updates. After browsing and selecting a PDF (for instance, a user guide for SpaceX's Falcon 9 rocket) and clicking "Add File", you should observe the spinner in action:

Chat with Document

Upload file:

Drag and drop file here
Limit 200MB per file • PDF, DOCX, TXT

Browse files

falcon-users-guide-2021-09.pdf 5.7MB ✕

Add File

Reading, chunking and embedding file...

Once the file is successfully uploaded, you can proceed with inquiries like "How many engines does the Falcon 9 rocket have?" and receive accurate answers:

Input your question

How many engines does the Falcon 9 rocket have?

The Falcon 9 rocket has nine engines in its first stage.

Question: How many engines does the Falcon 9 rocket have?

Answer: The Falcon 9 rocket has nine engines in its first stage.

Feel free to try this with a .doc file; it should work seamlessly.

With these enhancements, our chat-with-document app is more robust and versatile. It now supports multiple document types, connects to a language model, processes queries, and retains chat history for contextual awareness in subsequent interactions.

I hope you've gleaned valuable insights from this chapter. The potential applications span various fields, including legal, medical, scientific, and technical domains. The possibilities are boundless.

CHAPTER 15: CHAT WITH YOUTUBE

We already have our "question-answering chat with document" application. Now, we're going to make a small tweak to this app, allowing it to chat with a YouTube video. You're likely familiar with lengthy YouTube videos that can be time-consuming to watch. Imagine if you could directly ask questions about these videos to save time.

In this tutorial, we'll show that not only can you load data from documents, but you can also source data from platforms like YouTube, Wikipedia, and other online resources.

If we refer back to the LangChain documentation and the document loader section I mentioned earlier, you'll find an entry on how to load documents from Youtube transcripts (https://python.langchain.com/docs/integrations/document_loaders/youtube_transcript).

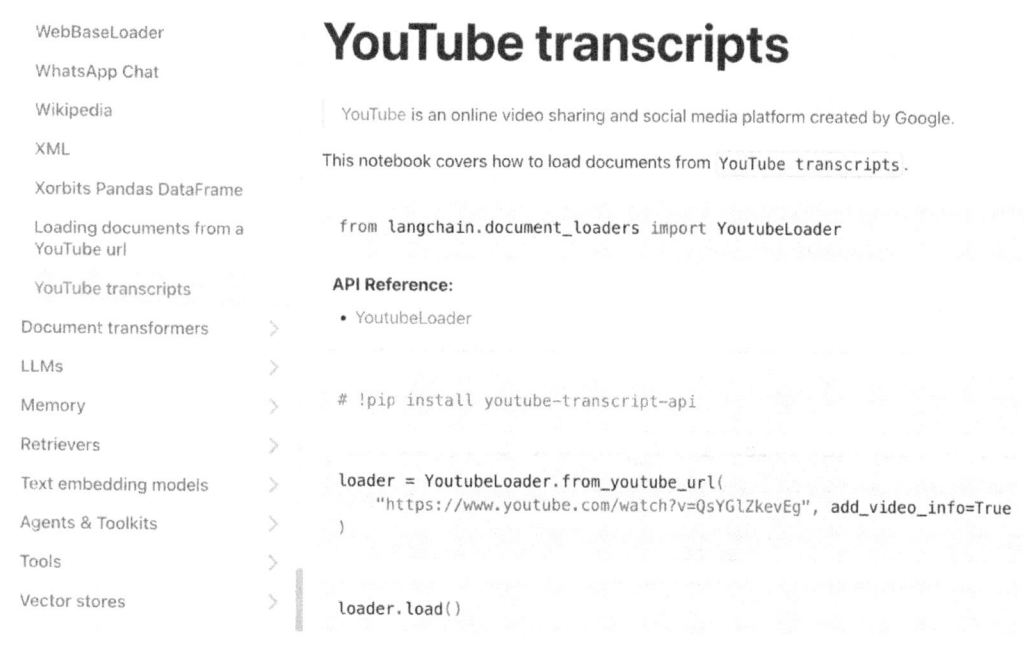

YouTube transcripts

YouTube is an online video sharing and social media platform created by Google.

This notebook covers how to load documents from `YouTube transcripts`.

```
from langchain.document_loaders import YoutubeLoader
```

API Reference:
- YoutubeLoader

```
# !pip install youtube-transcript-api
```

```
loader = YoutubeLoader.from_youtube_url(
    "https://www.youtube.com/watch?v=QsYGlZkevEg", add_video_info=True
)
```

```
loader.load()
```

We can utilize the YouTube loader, but first, we need to install the YouTube transcript API. You can easily install this by copying the given command and running it in your terminal.

```
pip install youtube-transcript-api==0.6.2
```

To avoid disturbing our current code, I've copied everything and pasted it into a new file named chat_youtube.py. Much of the original code remains untouched. But we no longer need the file upload functions, so those can be removed.

Given that we're loading from YouTube, there's no need to upload byte data anymore. We'll retain the session and chat history components.

chat_youtube.py will look something like (add the codes in **bold**):

```
import os
from apikey import apikey

import streamlit as st
from langchain_openai import ChatOpenAI
from langchain.text_splitter import RecursiveCharacterTextSplitter
from langchain_openai import OpenAIEmbeddings
from langchain_community.vectorstores import Chroma
from langchain.chains import ConversationalRetrievalChain
from langchain_community.document_loaders import YoutubeLoader

os.environ["OPENAI_API_KEY"] = apikey

def clear_history():
    if 'history' in st.session_state:
        del st.session_state['history']

st.title('Chat with ~~Document~~ Youtube')
youtube_url = st.text_input('Input your Youtube URL')

if youtube_url:
    loader = YoutubeLoader.from_youtube_url(youtube_url)
    documents = loader.load()

    text_splitter = RecursiveCharacterTextSplitter(chunk_size=1000, chunk_overlap=200)
        ...
        ...
```

Since the user will be providing a YouTube URL, we need an input field for that. We create an input field labeled "Input your YouTube URL". We then load the Youtube transcript with the user's Youtube URL input.

Running our App

Once everything's set up, we'll save and run the new chat_youtube.py file.

```
streamlit run chat_youtube.py
```

For demonstration purposes, let's use a familiar music video: "Never Gonna Give You Up."

After entering the video URL and letting the app process, you can ask a question like, "What am I never going to do?" The app should return something like: "you are never going to let someone down"

Chat with Youtube

Input your Youtube URL

https://www.youtube.com/watch?v=dQw4w9WgXcQ

File uploaded, chunked and embedded successfully

Input your question

What am I never going to do?

Based on the given context, you are never going to let someone down.

Question: What am I never going to do?

Answer: Based on the given context, you are never going to let someone down.

And yes, you've just been subtly "rickrolled"!

I hope you enjoyed this chapter and now understand how to load data from external sources as well.

In case you got lost, here's the entire code of chat_youtube.py:

```
import os
from apikey import apikey

import streamlit as st
from langchain_openai import ChatOpenAI
from langchain_community.text_splitter import RecursiveCharacterTextSplitter
from langchain_openai import OpenAIEmbeddings
from langchain_community.vectorstores import Chroma
from langchain.chains import ConversationalRetrievalChain
from langchain_community.document_loaders import YoutubeLoader

os.environ["OPENAI_API_KEY"] = apikey

def clear_history():
    if 'history' in st.session_state:
        del st.session_state['history']
```

```python
st.title('Chat with Youtube')
youtube_url = st.text_input('Input your Youtube URL')

if youtube_url:
    loader = YoutubeLoader.from_youtube_url(youtube_url)
    documents = loader.load()

    text_splitter = RecursiveCharacterTextSplitter(chunk_size=1000,
    chunk_overlap=200)
    chunks = text_splitter.split_documents(documents)
    embeddings = OpenAIEmbeddings()
    vector_store = Chroma.from_documents(chunks, embeddings)

    # initialize OpenAI instance
    llm = ChatOpenAI(model='gpt-3.5-turbo', temperature=0)
    retriever=vector_store.as_retriever()

    crc = ConversationalRetrievalChain.from_llm(llm, retriever)

    st.session_state.crc = crc

    # success message when file is chunked & embedded successfully
    st.success('File uploaded, chunked and embedded successfully')

# get question from user input
question = st.text_input('Input your question')

if question:
    if 'crc' in st.session_state:
        crc = st.session_state.crc

        if 'history' not in st.session_state:
            st.session_state['history'] = []

        response = crc.invoke({
            'question':question,
            'chat_history': st.session_state['history']
        })

        st.session_state['history'].append((question,response['answer']))
```

```
st.write(response['answer'])
for prompts in st.session_state ['history']:
    st.write("Question: " + prompts[0])
    st.write("Answer: " + prompts[1])
```

Final Words

We have gone through quite a lot of content to equip you with the skills to create LangChain LLM AI apps.

Hopefully, you have enjoyed this book and would like to learn more from me. I would love to get your feedback, learning what you liked and didn't for us to improve.

Please feel free to email me at support@i-ducate.com to get updated versions of this book.

If you didn't like the book, or if you feel that I should have covered certain additional topics, please email us to let us know. This book can only get better thanks to readers like you.

If you like the book, I would appreciate if you could leave us a review too. Thank you and all the best for your learning journey!

About the Author

Greg Lim is a technologist and author of several programming books. Greg has many years in teaching programming in tertiary institutions and he places special emphasis on learning by doing.

Contact Greg at support@i-ducate.com